MW00388466

The Saladmaster Guide to Healthy & Nutritious Cooking

from the kitchen of
SALADMASTER

• •

THE SUMMIT PUBLISHING GROUP • ARLINGTON, TEXAS

THE SUMMIT PUBLISHING GROUP
One Arlington Centre
1112 East Copeland Dr.
Fifth Floor
Arlington, Texas 76011

Copyright © 1995 by Saladmaster, Inc. All rights reserved. No part of this boo
may be reproduced, or transmitted in any form or by any means, electronic c
mechanical, including photocopying, recording or by any information storag
and retrieval system, without the written permission of the publisher, excep
where permitted by law.

Saladmaster

912 113th Street
Arlington, Texas 76011
1-800-765-5795

95 96 97 98 99   5 4 3 2 1

Library of Congress Cataloging-in-Publication Data

The Saladmaster guide to healthy & nutritious cooking : from the kitchen of
    Saladmaster.
        p. cm.
    ISBN 1-56530-186-2
    1. Steaming (Cookery) 2. Broiling. 3. Cookware. 4. Nutrition.
I. Saladmaster (Firm)
TX691.S25 1995
641.5'87—dc20   95-34643
                                                                CIP

Cover design by David Sims
Book design by John Baird

Cover photography by Lee Angle Photography, Inc.

Table of Contents

2. Soups and Stews

3. Vegetables

4. Vegetarian Main Dishes

5. Breakfast and Breads

6. Meats

9. Ethnic Dishes

10. Desserts

10. Other Saladmaster Products

Welcome to the Saladmaster Guide to Healthy and Nutritious Cooking

Congratulations on your choice of Saladmaster's System 7 cookware. You have made an investment in good health and nutrition. Your Saladmaster cookware will enable you to cook without added fat or water...for a lifetime.

What this means to you is maximum nutrition and flavor without unnecessary calories. It also means optimum retention of vitamins and minerals. Cooking the Saladmaster way enhances the basic flavors of healthful foods without adding salt, sugar, fats, or oils. You'll discover the true taste of foods.

Waterless cooking reduces cooking time, too. Certainly, that makes your work in the kitchen easier...and less time-consuming. Roasting or baking on top of the stove can cut in half the time it takes you laboring and sweating over a regular oven. Saladmaster's unique vapor-seal lids create a semi-vacuum. This shortens cooking time and keeps food warm long after the heat is turned off.

Now, you might be curious to know why our line of cookware is called Saladmaster. Interesting story. The original Saladmaster machine, simple to use and easy to store, was our company's first product. This handy shredder and slicer has repeatedly proven itself over the years. The success of its innovative design created a demand for cookware as functional as the Saladmaster. With nutrition, convenience, and economy always primary considerations, we developed cookware equal in quality.

Saladmaster utensils are state of the art. Inner layers of aluminum and alloys promote radiant heat conduction. Outer layers of surgical stainless steel promote easy cleanup and lasting beauty.

Before you begin cooking with your new Saladmaster System 7, please read and follow the instructions for use and care of the utensils. Consider this cookbook your user's manual. Our easy-to-follow directions will quickly enable you to get the most out of your new equipment.

The book's introduction will explain everything you need to know about using Saladmaster cookware, complete with step-by-step instructions, uses for each piece of equipment, photos depicting the cookware, healthful food replacements, etc. That is followed by the cooking section, which consists of more than one hundred sixty recipes divided among ten categories of eating preference.

Each of these ten "chapters" begins with a short overview of the recipes to follow, and include some basic techniques for everyday cooking. Next you'll find a tasty collection of contemporary recipes selected for convenience, ease, nutritional value, and good taste—without added fat. Also sprinkled throughout the book are dozens of special cooking tips—we call them sidebars—that will help make you a Saladmaster chef in no time. As an added bonus, we have also included a nutritional analysis for each recipe, as analyzed by a certified nutritionist. No doubt you will find this information invaluable.

By following our simple, clear instructions and proven recipes, you will quickly learn the waterless techniques for the ultimate in healthful cooking, using some of the most carefully designed cookware on the market today.

What You Need to Know about the Saladmaster Health and Nutrition Cooking System

By following the techniques recommended for your new Saladmaster cookware, you will be able to eat healthier and, in many cases, cook faster than traditional methods.

The special design of our cookware preserves vital nutrients through efficient heat distribution. The unique Vapo-Valve eliminates guesswork by signaling when to turn down heat, thus creating a vapor seal that allows cooking without water or fat.

Saladmaster Features and Benefits:

- Vapo-Valve takes the guesswork out of waterless cooking.

- 304-316 surgical stainless steel, the highest quality available, preserves the mirror finish for years with a minimum of care.

- multiradiant core for even heat distribution on the bottom and sides —allows you to "bake" on top of the stove

- wide, dripless pouring edge

- cool pistol-grip handles and knobs for safety—and ovenproof to 400 degrees

- rounded corners prevent food and grease buildup, for easier cleaning.

- self-nesting lids for easy storage

- waterless cooking preserves nutrition and enhances foods' flavor.

Getting Started

Before first use:
Wash each piece of new Saladmaster cookware in your sink, using hot, soapy water that contains 1 cup vinegar. This removes all traces of manufacturing oils and polishing compounds. Rinse in clear, hot water and dry well with a clean, non-abrasive towel.

Daily-use cleaning:
Wash in hot, soapy water, rinse and dry; or clean in dishwasher (avoid the heat-dry setting).

For stubborn stains or stuck-on food:
Rinse pan and sprinkle with mild stainless-steel cleanser, such as Saladmaster Glo that comes with your cookware. To purchase more, contact your Saladmaster representative or phone 1-800-765-5795. *Never use steel wool or hard abrasives on the outside of your cookware as they might dull the finish.*

Using Your New Saladmaster Cookware

Is As Easy as 1-2-3.
1. Use the correct-size pan—at least two-thirds filled with food.

2. Preheat pan for meats and poultry over medium heat, or start with a cold, dry pan for fruits and vegetables.

3. Listen for the clicking of the Vapo-Valve. When the valve clicks, reduce heat to low so that clicking stops. Cook according to recipe instructions or desired doneness.

Tips for Use

1. Never use high heat. All you need to know are medium and low! Preheat pans over medium heat, according to your electric range setting. If necessary, use lower settings to control temperature. When using a gas stove, heat is medium when the flame reaches halfway to the bottom of the pan. When the Vapo-Valve clicks, turn the heat to low. On an electric range, that might be as low as your stove can go. On a gas range, heat is low at the lowest flame without going out. If your lowest flame is still too high, use a heat-reducing ring or pad on your burner.

2. Do not put salt directly on surface of pans. When using salt, make sure it dissolves completely to avoid leaving white spots. *Beware: Salt could even pit surfaces.*

3. Preheating usually takes three to five minutes. To tell when a pan is properly preheated, splash a few drops of water on the surface. If the drops bead and dance, the pan is preheated. Or, lay a paper towel in the pan. When the towel turns brown, the pan is properly preheated.

Stack Cooking

Have You Ever Needed Just One More Burner?

Stack cooking can provide that extra burner you need, thus allowing you to prepare two or more dishes while utilizing just one burner. The Saladmaster System is specifically designed to provide even heat distribution and the vacuum seal required for stack cooking.

First, start your food on medium heat. When the Vapo-Valve clicks, simply turn off the burner and then "stack" the pan on top of one that is already cooking over another burner. Thanks to the built-in seven layers that evenly conduct heat across the bottom, up the sides and through the cover, each piece of cookware becomes a little oven of its own, with the top piece of cookware becoming nearly as hot as the bottom piece.

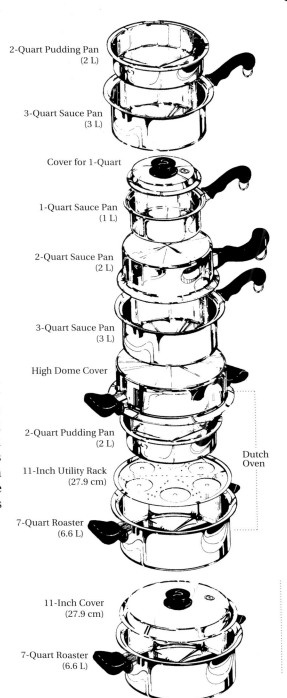

2-Quart Pudding Pan
(2 L)

3-Quart Sauce Pan
(3 L)

Cover for 1-Quart

1-Quart Sauce Pan
(1 L)

2-Quart Sauce Pan
(2 L)

3-Quart Sauce Pan
(3 L)

High Dome Cover

2-Quart Pudding Pan
(2 L)

11-Inch Utility Rack
(27.9 cm)

7-Quart Roaster
(6.6 L)

Dutch Oven

11-Inch Cover
(27.9 cm)

7-Quart Roaster
(6.6 L)

Stack Cooking

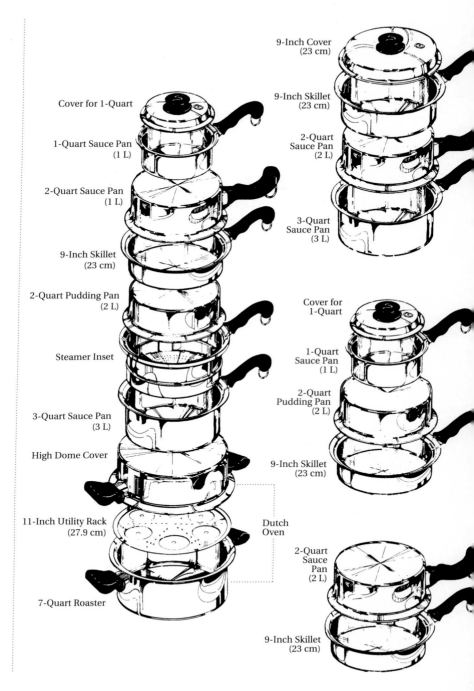

9-Inch Cover
(23 cm)

9-Inch Skillet
(23 cm)

2-Quart
Sauce Pan
(2 L)

3-Quart
Sauce Pan
(3 L)

Cover for 1-Quart

1-Quart Sauce Pan
(1 L)

2-Quart Sauce Pan
(1 L)

9-Inch Skillet
(23 cm)

2-Quart Pudding Pan
(2 L)

Steamer Inset

3-Quart Sauce Pan
(3 L)

High Dome Cover

Cover for
1-Quart

1-Quart
Sauce Pan
(1 L)

2-Quart
Pudding Pan
(2 L)

9-Inch Skillet
(23 cm)

11-Inch Utility Rack
(27.9 cm)

Dutch
Oven

7-Quart Roaster

2-Quart
Sauce
Pan
(2 L)

9-Inch Skillet
(23 cm)

Stack Cooking

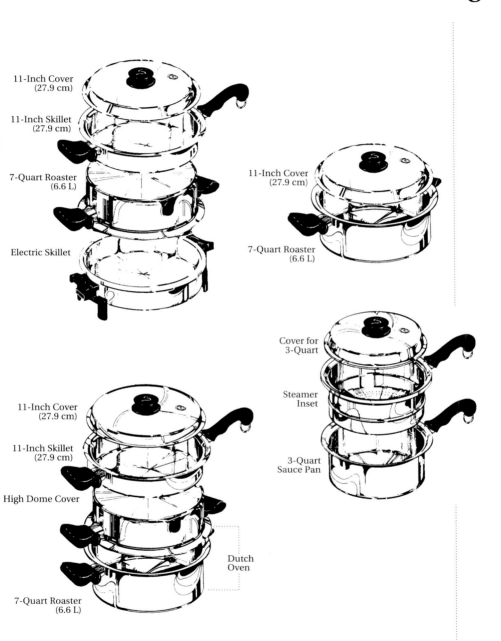

11-Inch Cover
(27.9 cm)

11-Inch Skillet
(27.9 cm)

7-Quart Roaster
(6.6 L)

Electric Skillet

11-Inch Cover
(27.9 cm)

7-Quart Roaster
(6.6 L)

Cover for
3-Quart

Steamer
Inset

3-Quart
Sauce Pan

11-Inch Cover
(27.9 cm)

11-Inch Skillet
(27.9 cm)

High Dome Cover

Dutch
Oven

7-Quart Roaster
(6.6 L)

Which Piece Should You Use and for What?

Here's a rundown of utensils in the Saladmaster set. You're using the right size if it's at least two-thirds' full.

■ 7-quart Dutch oven

Ideal base utensil for stack cooking. Use the High Dome cover for a Dutch oven and the 11-inch cover for soups, stews, etc. It's great for turkeys and large roasts.

■ 3-quart saucepan

Good for bulky vegetables, such as corn on the cob or a pan full of cabbage. If you use the Steamer Inset, you can have steaming fresh or frozen

KEY

A. 2-Quart Pudding Pan (2L)

B. 2-Quart Steamer Inset (2L) *fits 3-Quart Sauce Pan*

C. 9-Inch Skillet with Cover (23cm)

D. 1-Quart Sauce Pan with Cover (1L)

E. 3-Quart Sauce Pan with Cover (3L)

F. Six Egg Cups

G. 7-Quart Roaster with High Dome Cover (6.6L) (Dutch Oven)

H. 11-Inch Skillet with Cover (27.9cm)

I. 2-Quart Sauce Pan with Cover (2L)

J. 11-Inch Utility Rack (27.9cm)

vegetables in no time. You might also try putting one food—such as sauerkraut—in the 3-quart saucepan and hot dogs in the steamer, preparing them both at the same time.

■ 2-quart saucepan

Also called the family pan because it holds 4 to 8 servings of vegetables, potatoes, or fruits such as applesauce.

■ 1-quart saucepan

Works well for simultaneously cooking two 10-ounce packages of frozen vegetables. The cookware will hold more of your food of choice because you don't need to add water.

■ Large skillet

Multiple steaks, chops, large meat loaf, greaseless fried chicken, skillet suppers. Use with 11-inch cover or High Dome for small roasts. Also a good base for stack cooking.

■ Small skillet

A couple of steaks, chops or chicken breasts, small meat loaf, stovetop baking, and vegetables. Invert the pudding pan and use as a small roaster for meats such as eye of round or pork loin.

■ Steamer inset

Quick-cook vegetables or remove grease from ground beef or sausages. Also use to steam-heat leftovers, buns, rice, or pasta. Also use as a drainer, strainer, or colander.

■ Utility racks

Handy separators for stack cooking. Use the 6-cup rack with the 7-quart Dutch oven or large skillet, and the 4-cup rack with the 3-quart saucepan or small skillet. This is really great for cooking corn on the cob.

■ Utility cups

Warm baby foods individually while cooking your food underneath; melt butter or chocolate; bake muffins, biscuits, or cornbread on top of the stove; poach eggs. Use with 6-cup or 4-cup racks over 1-inch of water in appropriate-size pan (see utility racks above).

■ Pudding pan

Bake cakes or puddings inside the large skillet or 7-quart Dutch oven; just place on utility rack and use the dome lid. May also be used as double boiler, or inverted and used as a high-dome cover for the 3-quart saucepan or the small skillet. Handle carefully because this utensil does not have handles.

Using the Saladmaster Machine

This handy, simple-to-use machine is the original Saladmaster product. It allows precision slicing of vegetables; fruits; nuts; crackers; cheese; hard sausage; cooked, pickled, or smoked fish or shrimp.

Easy to turn, this manually operated food cutter allows you to have complete control over the speed of the device and size of the pieces of food.

To use:

1. Remove the food guide cover by sliding it away from the opening. Do not try to lift off.
2. Select the correct cone for the cutting job. (See descriptions that follow.)
3. Insert cone into locking mechanism opposite the handle.
4. Turn to make sure handle turns and cone is secure.
5. Cut pieces of food so they will slide through the opening.
6. Position machine so that suction cups attach it securely to countertop.
7. Place a bowl directly under the slicing cone to catch food.
8. Hold palm flat against the top of the food. Push food through using constant pressure, while turning the handle to activate the cutting mechanism.
   Caution: The blades are very sharp. Do not place fingers in the opening while cone is in place.
9. Wash base well in warm, soapy water. Drain or towel dry. Replace the food guide cover and store. Shredding and cutting cones should not be placed in dishwasher.

Numbers stamped on the base of each cone indicate the type and function of each blade:

■ No. 1—Shredder

For any food that you desire shredded very fine, or for grating any hard foods such as cheese, dry bread, crackers, or nuts.

- **Beets/carrots/turnips/potatoes**—Do not peel. The most plentiful amounts of mineral salts and vitamins are contained in their skins or just under the skins. The shredder cutting cone will prepare food so that peeling or scraping is unnecessary.

● **Crackers/dry bread**—Fill hopper and grate. Use crumbs for icebox pies, fish, or oyster dishes.

● **Celery**—Shredded celery is excellent for soup or salad dressings. Place string side toward hopper to eliminate strings.

● **Frozen foods**—Shred frozen fruits while still frozen for sundaes, desserts, etc.

■ No. 2—Stringer

For cutting foods into medium-size "strings." Cuts considerably larger than shredder, but smaller than french fryer.

● **Onions**—Remove skin and cut onions in half for best results, placing outside of onion next to the hopper.

● **Carrots**—Do not peel carrots. Cut into shoestrings for salads and waterless cooking.

● **Soft cheese**—Stringer cuts soft cheese into "macaroni-size"…perfect for salads or cooking. Cheese cut this way may be used for flavoring other dishes.

● **Apples**—To peel apples or other fruits, place peeling side to hopper. Serve apple with peel left on for more healthful, appetizing, and eye-appealing dish.

■ No. 3—French Fryer

Designed for potatoes and other firm vegetables which become the perfect size for fast cooking.

● **Carrots/beets/turnips**—Cuts carrots and turnips perfectly for waterless cooking. This French fryer is also the cutting cone to use for beets when you want to prepare them for canning.

● **Fruits**—Fresh pears, apples, or peaches can now be attractively prepared. Apples are excellent for Waldorf salads and apple pies, with each slice having an eye-catching "peeling" tip for decoration.

● **Melons**—Cut melons, papayas, and avocados into quarters or eighths and feed them into the hopper with skin away from the cutter.

■ No. 4—Thin Slicer

Used for preparing potato chips, carrot curls, coleslaw, or any other food to be thinly sliced.

- **Radishes/carrots**—Fill hopper full of radishes and press firmly with palm of hand. For carrot curls, lay carrot flat across cutting cone and press firmly.
- **Onions/pickles**—For hamburgers or sandwiches where very thin slices are desired. Best results are obtained if onion is skinned, cut in half, and outside is placed next to cutting cone.
- **Sauerkraut/slaw**—The proper cut for coleslaw and sauerkraut is delicate, lacy shreds. Cut cabbage in halves or quarters and remove the heart. Always cut the cabbage with the leafy side toward the cone.

■ No. 5—Waffler

Used for making fancy waffled cuts of either fruits or vegetables. This cone does not cut as thinly as does the thin slicer.

- **Potatoes**—Do not peel. Simply cut and fry to a golden brown. Sweet potatoes, which must first be peeled, also are excellent when waffled.
- **Apples**—Cut apple in half and remove core. Slice, cook, and serve. For pickled beets, cook, slice, and then pickle. Excellent for canning.
- **Bananas**—Slice for fruit salads. Fast and attractive.
- **Carrots**—Do not peel. Slice, cook, and season. Very decorative for salads.

Knowing Your Cookware

Here are a few other tips to keep in mind as you enjoy many years of using your Saladmaster cookware:

● As much as you will love using your new Saladmaster cookware, you will also appreciate knowing that your cookware, like sterling or fine wines, actually improves with age. With your new set, you can assume there will be a breaking-in process that takes about two or three months, during which your cookware becomes more and more efficient.

● It is possible that one of your pieces of cookware will turn blue on the bottom, or even on the inside. Don't panic. This appearance of blue means only that a high heat has been used for an excessive amount of time. You can scorch anything, even Saladmaster cookware, simply by using a high heat. If this does occur, rest assured that it will eventually fade away. Remember, you haven't hurt the cookware in this instance; you have simply burned the metal. It is still sanitary and will cook as efficiently and safely. Keep in mind: **It is never necessary to set your burner to the highest heat, even when boiling water**.

● Sometimes, a white film will appear on the inside bottom of your cookware. This is, primarily, sodium cooked out of foods and calcium deposits that dishwater won't get out. Your Saladmaster Glo will take care of it. Likewise, any burnt-on grease or carbon deposits on the bottom of your cookware will disappear with your cleanser. Your cleaner is used to polish your cookware. Remember: Saladmaster Glo.

We also recommend using a damp paper towel with the cleanser because a paper towel is abrasive enough to clean the cookware all over without scratching the sides or top of the lids, which are polished to an extremely high sheen. You may use anything on the inside bottom, even a mixer. You will scratch it, but you will not hurt the cooking ability of the cookware.

Saladmaster is made to be used, not pampered. To keep the cookware looking pretty on the outside (because that is what people will notice) never use an abrasive on the outside finish. If you want to use an S.O.S. pad on the inside, feel free to do so—but not on the outside. If anything sticks, add hot water and let set for 10 minutes.

● **Never put cold water in a hot pan**. Even as thick and heavy as Saladmaster cookware is, cold water in a hot pan could warp the cookware. Let the pan cool down first and then add warm water.

Healthful Replacements for Commonly Used Foods

Commonly Used Food	Healthful Replacement
Bread crumbs, white	Wheat germ; whole-grain bread crumbs
Butter	Low-fat margarine; cholesterol-free vegetable oil
Corn flakes	Wheat germ; crushed whole-grain bread crumbs
Cream, sour or whipped	Yogurt
Cream cheese for spreading	Make your own from yogurt
Flour, white, as a thickener	Whole wheat flour; cornstarch; soft-cooked rice
Gelatin, artificially flavored and sweetened	Unflavored, unsweetened gelatin
Lard	Low-salt butter or margarine; vegetable oil
Milk, whole	Low-fat or skim milk; low-fat yogurt
Pancake syrup, commercial	Honey; molasses; pure maple syrup
Pasta, white	Whole wheat pasta
Rice, white	Brown rice; bulgur
Salt	Herbs; spices; lemon juice; wine (alcohol evaporates in cooking)
Shortening, hydrogenated	Low-salt butter or margarine; vegetable oil
Soups, canned cream	Chicken broth, powdered milk, and pureed vegetables
Sugar, brown or white	Fruit juice; honey; maple syrup; molasses

Questions? Here are some answers.

1. Can I put Saladmaster cookware in the dishwasher?

A. *Yes. After time, however, repeated washing in the dishwasher may dull the handles. It is strongly recommended that the heat-dry cycle be avoided when using Saladmaster in the dishwasher. Use the energy-efficient air-dry cycle.*

2. After I've lowered the heat and the seal has formed, can I lift the lid?

A. *Peek if you must. After replacing the lid, spin it so that the Vapo-Valve clicks, indicating that it has re-sealed itself. If it does not, increase heat until the valve clicks, then reduce heat to low.*

3. What if my range cooks at too high a temperature?

A. *If your lowest temperature is still too high, you may need to purchase a heat-reducing pad for your burner, such as the type used under glass coffee pots on electric stoves.*

4. Can I ever cook over high heat?

A. *High heat may cause warping. Also, foods are more likely to stick or scorch over high heat and cooking at a too high heat can cause food to shrink and dry. It is okay, however, to bring large amounts of liquid to a boil, such as water for pasta, over high heat. Lower heat after boiling point has been reached.*

5. Can I carve a roast in the pan?

A. *Never use sharp utensils to cut foods in the pan to avoid damaging the finish.*

6. Why does the Vapo-Valve click as soon as I turn the heat on under a covered pan? Should I lower the heat at that time?

A. *The Vapo-Valve is designed to click when the food or liquid inside the pan reaches approximately 185 degrees. Occasionally, slow clicking does begin before the pan has been exposed to heat long enough to reach that level. When that happens, proceed as you would without the premature click. The click should stop as the heat rises. Once the temperature hits approximately 185 degrees, the Vapo-Valve will click again. This time, the click will be more rapid and insistent. Then it is time to turn down the heat under the pan.*

If you have other questions, please contact your Saladmaster dealer or representative, or call this toll-free number, **1-800-765-5795**; or contact our headquarters: **Saladmaster, Inc.,**® 912 113th Street, Arlington, Texas, 76011.

The Food Guide Pyramid

Often, what's new is actually quite old, and so it is with the U.S. Department of Agriculture's release of the Food Guide Pyramid in 1992. This symbol represents a diet with more whole grains, breads, fruits, and vegetables, and less fats, oils and sugar. Not surprisingly, the eating plan is similar to what scientists believe human diets were like in simpler times and in some cultures today, particularly in the Mediterranean region.

A healthful diet should include 6 to 11 daily servings of bread, cereal, rice, or pasta; 2 to 4 servings of fruit; 3 to 5 vegetable servings; 2 to 3 servings of milk, yogurt or cheese (preferably low fat); and 2 to 3 servings of meat, poultry, fish, dry beans, eggs, or nuts. Fats, oils, and sweets should be used sparingly. Also important, say health experts, is to eat a diet from which 30 percent of the total calories come from fat. The typical American diet is closer to 40 percent calories from fat.

KEY

● Fat (naturally occuring and added

▲ Sugars (added)

These symbols show that fat and added sugars come mostly from fats, oils, and sweets, but can be a part of or added to foods from the other food groups as well.

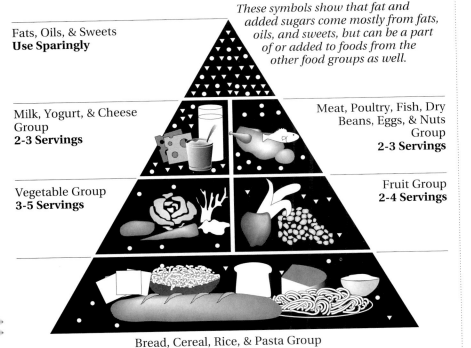

Fats, Oils, & Sweets
Use Sparingly

Milk, Yogurt, & Cheese
Group
2-3 Servings

Meat, Poultry, Fish, Dry Beans, Eggs, & Nuts
Group
2-3 Servings

Vegetable Group
3-5 Servings

Fruit Group
2-4 Servings

Bread, Cereal, Rice, & Pasta Group
6-11 Servings

Nutritional Information

The nutritional analysis, which follows each recipe, is based on the largest number of servings specified in the recipe. Where choices are provided, an asterisk (*) is placed next to the choice used in the analysis.

Each recipe has been analyzed for its number of calories per largest serving; grams of protein, fat, carbohydrate, and fiber; and milligrams of cholesterol and sodium.

Eggplant Dip with Stuffed Tiny Red Potatoes

Appetizers and Salads

Selecting nutritious, tasty appetizers can be a real challenge. But there are many choices beyond greasy, salt-laden chips with high-fat dips. Vegetables, salsas, marinated seafood, vegetable-based dips—all these can make tasty munchies without breaking your diet resolve.

Of course, preparing your own appetizers and snacks can be a big money-saving measure as well. Often easy to assemble, these tasty recipes reflect current taste and nutrition trends.

Many recipes make excellent use of new low- and nonfat products, including cheeses, sour cream, and yogurt.

Variety is the key when selecting appetizers. Some should be full-flavored or spicy, like hot chicken wings or marinated shrimp. Provide lots of vegetable snacks, like eggplant dip with carrot, celery, and squash dippers, and stuffed new potatoes.

It is possible to make a meal of appetizers with a selection of salads and finger foods.

Salads can be one-dish meals as well as tasty accompaniments to a meal. Remember that nutrition experts recommend at least five servings per day of fruits and vegetables. Serving a salad along with the meal can help achieve this nutritional goal.

Fiesta Taco Salad

Utensils: Small skillet, Saladmaster Machine
Yield: 6-8 servings

4	ounces reduced-fat or *fat-free cheddar cheese
1	medium onion
1	pound extra lean ground beef
1	(1 1/4-ounce) package taco sauce mix
3/4	cup water
1	(7-ounce) package nacho cheese tortilla chips; or baked tortilla chips
1	head lettuce
3	medium tomatoes; chopped

Process cheese using #1 cone, onion using #2 cone.

Preheat skillet on medium heat, add meat, brown and drain. Add onion, taco sauce mix and water, reduce heat to low; simmer 5 minutes. Refrigerate until cool.

While meat is cooling, tear lettuce into bite size pieces, place in large salad bowl. Add meat, tomatoes and cheese. Slightly crush chips, add to salad, toss gently.

Serve with your favorite dressing.

1 serving contains:

Cal	Prot	Fat	Carb	Fiber	Chol	Sodium
318	21.4 g	17.5 g	19.9 g	2.3 g	51.9 mg	334 mg

Saladmaster Fruit Salad

Utensil: Saladmaster Machine;
Yield: 6-8 servings

1	medium lemon
1	medium orange
1/2	cup pecans
3	large apples, cored
4	medium bananas
1	(8-ounce) can crushed pineapple; undrained

Grate lemon and orange rinds and chop pecans using #1 cone. Process apples using #3 cone, bananas using #5 cone.

Remove membrane from orange and lemon, separate into sections. Place in a large bowl, add apples, bananas, pineapple and pecans. Sprinkle with all of grated orange and lemon rind.

1 serving contains:

Cal	Prot	Fat	Carb	Fiber	Chol	Sodium
129	1.5 g	5.4 g	21.8 g	2.5 g	0 mg	1 mg

Health Salad

Utensil: Saladmaster Machine
Yield: 6-8 servings

2	ounces reduced-fat or *fat-free cheddar cheese
1	medium carrot
1/3	head green cabbage
1/4	head red cabbage
3	radishes
1/2	medium cucumber

Process cheese, carrot and cabbages using #1 cone, radishes and cucumber using #4 cone.

Place all ingredients in bowl. Serve with your choice of salad dressing.

1 serving contains:

Cal	Prot	Fat	Carb	Fiber	Chol	Sodium
22.4	2.8 g	0.1 g	3.1 g	1.1 g	1.3 mg	59 mg

Easy melon salad

Using a melon baller, scoop red watermelon and cantaloupe balls into a large salad bowl. Or you may use the scooped-out half of the watermelon as the salad bowl. Be sure and scallop the bowl's edges. Thaw a small can of limeade in the refrigerator. Pour limeade, undiluted, over melon balls, stirring to coat evenly. Refrigerate until ready to serve.

Black-Eyed Pea Salad

Utensils: 3-quart saucepan, Saladmaster Machine
Yield: 6 servings

10	**cups water, divided**
2	**cups dry black-eyed peas**
1/4	**medium onion**
1/2	**medium green pepper**
2	**tablespoons finely chopped canned jalapeno peppers**
2	**tablespoons canola or *olive oil**
2	**tablespoons red wine vinegar**
1	**clove garlic, minced**
1/4	**teaspoon freshly ground black pepper**

Pour 6 cups water in saucepan, add peas; soak overnight. Drain and rinse, add 4 cups water; cook over low heat 1 1/2 hours. Rinse in cold water, drain.

Process onion and green pepper using #2 cone.

In bowl combine onion, pepper and all remaining ingredients; mix well, add peas; chill 1 hour.

1 serving contains:

Cal	Prot	Fat	Carb	Fiber	Chol	Sodium
234	13.3 g	5.3 g	35 g	15.4 g	0 mg	51 mg

Shortcut: Drain 4 cans black-eyed peas and proceed as with cooked peas. For fresher flavor, use frozen black-eyed peas. In season, buy "a mess" of peas at a farmer's market and enjoy this delicious salad using fresh-cooked black-eyed peas.

Seasonal color

Depending on the season, add color to salads with the following:
Summer: blueberries, raspberries, cherries
Fall: pomegranate seeds
Winter: pink grapefruit
Spring: strawberries

Fresh Spinach Salad with Apple

Utensils: 1-quart saucepan, Saladmaster Machine
Yield: 10 servings

1	**large apple**
1	**celery stalk**
1	**pound fresh spinach**
1	**tablespoon lemon juice**
1/4	**cup balsamic vinegar**
1/4	**cup olive oil**
2	**teaspoons honey**
1	**teaspoon caraway seeds**

Process apple using #3 cone, celery using #4 cone.

Wash, dry, and remove stems from spinach; tear into bite-size pieces. Combine spinach, apple and celery in a large bowl. Sprinkle with lemon juice; toss well.

Combine vinegar, oil, honey, and caraway seeds in saucepan. Bring to boil over medium heat. Pour liquid over spinach mixture; toss well. Serve immediately.

1 serving contains:

Cal	Prot	Fat	Carb	Fiber	Chol	Sodium
72.9	1.5 g	5.6 g	5.7 g	1.6 g	0 mg	35.5 mg

Marinated Cucumber Salad

Utensil: Saladmaster Machine
Yield: 4 servings

2-3	**medium cucumbers**
1/4	**teaspoon salt substitute**
1/3	**cup vinegar**
3	**tablespoons sugar**
1	**tablespoon water**

Slice cucumbers using #5 Waffler cone.

Place cucumber slices in a medium bowl; sprinkle with salt substitute. In a small bowl combine vinegar, sugar and water; stir until sugar dissolves. Pour over cucumber slices. Cover and refrigerate until chilled.

Marinated Cucumber Salad, Cont.

1 serving contains:						
Cal	Prot	Fat	Carb	Fiber	Chol	Sodium
68	1.2 g	0.3 g	17.1 g	2.4 g	0 mg	4.5 mg

Water project: When time allows, sprinkle cucumber slices with salt substitute or salt and allow to sit for 30 minutes to an hour. Place cucumber slices in double thickness of cheesecloth or clean dish towel and squeeze to remove liquid. Slices should appear wilted. Combine cucumber slices with dressing and refrigerate several hours or overnight. For extra punch, add a small onion, sliced very thin, and a few sprigs of fresh dill.

Barbecue Chicken Wings

You'd have a difficult time finding a Texan who hasn't eaten a lot of barbecued chicken wings. Many Southwestern restaurants have started featuring them as an all-around favorite.

Utensil: Electric Skillet or Large Skillet
Yield:8-10 servings

2	pounds chicken winglets
1	18-ounce bottle barbecue sauce
1/8	teaspoon cayenne pepper

If using whole wings, remove small pointed ends.
Preheat electric skillet to 400 degrees or large skillet over medium-high heat. Add chicken, cook on each side for 10 minutes; remove, drain off any excess liquids.
In a small bowl mix sauce and pepper. Pour 1/2 sauce into skillet, add chicken, then pour remaining sauce over all. Simmer for 25 minutes.

1 serving contains:						
Cal	Prot	Fat	Carb	Fiber	Chol	Sodium
260	21.4 g	16.5 g	4.9 g	0.3 g	63.5 mg	477 mg

Waldorf Salad

A favorite for generations, this colorful salad is great to serve at both casual and elegant functions.

Utensil: Saladmaster Machine;
Yield: 8 servings

4	**celery stalks**
1	**medium golden apple, cored**
1	**medium red apple, cored**
1/2	**cup raisins**
1/2	**cup warm water**
1/2	**cup plain *reduced-fat or *fat-free yogurt**
1/4	**cup reduced-fat or *fat-free mayonnaise**
1/4	**cup buttermilk**
1	**cup seedless green grapes; halved**

Process celery using #2 cone, apples using #4 cone.

In a small bowl combine raisins and warm water; set aside 30 minutes to plump, then drain. Combine yogurt, mayonnaise and buttermilk in a blender; process until smooth.

In a large salad bowl combine fruit, celery and raisins.
Drizzle dressing over salad, toss lightly, cover and refrigerate until chilled.

● ●

1 serving contains:

Cal	Prot	Fat	Carb	Fiber	Chol	Sodium
84.4	1.7 g	0.6 g	20.6 g	2 g	1.2 mg	99.8 mg

● ●

Coleslaw with Fruit

This recipe's popularity has made it a standard in Saladmaster dinner parties for decades.

Utensil: Saladmaster Machine
Yield: 4 servings

1	medium carrot
3	medium apples, cored
1/3	head cabbage
1	(16-ounce) can pineapple tidbits, drained

Process carrot using #1 cone, apples and cabbage using #2 cone.
 Combine all ingredients in a medium bowl. Before serving, toss with coleslaw dressing (below).

1 serving contains:

Cal	Prot	Fat	Carb	Fiber	Chol	Sodium
165	1.4 g	1.1 g	41.8 g	7 g	0 mg	15 mg

Coleslaw Dressing No. 1

1/4	cup cider vinegar
1/2	cup sugar
1	cup reduced-fat or *fat-free mayonnaise or salad dressing

Blend all ingredients in a small bowl, pour over salad, cover, and refrigerate.

1 serving contains:

Cal	Prot	Fat	Carb	Fiber	Chol	Sodium
130	0 g	0 g	37.8 g	0 g	0 mg	501 mg

Coleslaw Dressing No. 2

6	tablespoons cider vinegar
1/4	cup honey
2	tablespoons reduced-fat or *fat-free mayonnaise

Blend all ingredients in a small bowl, pour over salad, cover, and refrigerate.

Coleslaw with Fruit

• •

1 serving contains:

Cal	Prot	Fat	Carb	Fiber	Chol	Sodium
71.1	0.1 g	0 g	20.3 g	0 g	0 mg	63.8 mg

• •

Coleslaw Dressing No. 3
  1/3   cup cider vinegar
  1/3   cup sugar
  1   cup reduced-fat or *fat-free salad dressing

Blend all ingredients in a small bowl, pour over salad, cover and refrigerate.

• •

1 serving contains:

Cal	Prot	Fat	Carb	Fiber	Chol	Sodium
97.9	0 g	0 g	29.6 g	0 g	0 mg	501 mg

• •

Orange juice dressing

This easy dressing goes well with the vegetable health salad or equally well with a combination of mandarin oranges, halved cherry tomatoes, green onions, and torn lettuce.
For the dressing, combine 1/4 cup orange juice, 2 teaspoons red wine vinegar, 1 tablespoon vegetable oil, and 2 teaspoons honey.

Chicken-Stuffed Mushrooms

Utensils: Saladmaster Machine, large skillet, 1-quart saucepan
Yield: 8 servings

1	**small onion**
4	**boneless, chicken breast halves, skinned**
	vegetable spray
16	**medium, fresh mushrooms**
2	**tablespoons margarine**
1	**slice bread; torn into small pieces**
2	**tablespoons cooking sherry**
1/4	**teaspoon marjoram**
1/8	**teaspoon freshly ground black pepper**
1/8	**teaspoon oregano**

Process onion using #2 cone.

Remove excess fat from chicken; chop into very small pieces. Spray skillet with vegetable spray, preheat over medium-high setting; add chicken, cook quickly until brown and tender; remove and set aside. Preheat broiler.

Clean mushrooms with vegetable brush, remove stems and chop; save mushroom caps.

In skillet melt 1 tablespoon margarine over medium-high heat. Add mushroom stems and onion; cook until tender. Add bread, sherry, marjoram, pepper, oregano and chicken.

In saucepan melt remaining margarine at medium-low heat. Place mushroom caps, round-side up, on cookie sheet; brush with melted margarine, broil 2 minutes; remove from oven. Invert mushroom caps; fill with chicken mixture. Brush with remaining melted margarine, broil 3 minutes.

• •
1 serving contains:

Cal	Prot	Fat	Carb	Fiber	Chol	Sodium
98.7	13.6 g	2.2 g	5.1 g	1.3 g	32.5 mg	54.1 mg

• •

Thick & Chewy Electric Skillet Pizza

This easy snack demonstrates the versatility of the electric skillet.

Utensils: Electric skillet, Saladmaster Machine;
Yield: 4 servings

10	ounces reduced-fat or *fat free mozzarella cheese
1/4	pound *Italian sausage, or reduced-fat turkey sausage
	prepared pizza dough
5	tablespoons pizza sauce
10	pepperoni slices

Process cheese using #2 cone.
Preheat skillet at 325 degrees. Add sausage; cook until no longer pink; remove and drain; set aside. Let skillet cool. Place dough in bottom of skillet; shape to fit pan. Spread pizza sauce over dough, top sauce with cheese, evenly distribute sausage and pepperoni slices over cheese. Cover; cook 10 minutes at 325 degrees. Turn unit off; let stand 10-15 minutes. (Note: DO NOT LIFT LID DURING COOKING TIME.)

1 serving contains:

Cal	Prot	Fat	Carb	Fiber	Chol	Sodium
453	37.6 g	16.3 g	37.8 g	1 g	39.4 mg	1544 mg

Layered Mexican Dip

A wonderful easy-to-prepare, carry-and-serve dip for "covered dish" parties; or serve it alone as a casserole.

Utensil: Electric skillet, Saladmaster Machine
Yield: 12 servings

1	small onion
6	ounces reduced-fat or *fat-free mozzarella cheese
4	ounces reduced-fat or *fat-free cheddar cheese
	vegetable spray
1/4	pound extra lean ground beef
2	(16-ounce) cans *fat-free refried beans
1	(4 to 5-ounce) can chopped green chilies
1	(8-ounce) jar taco sauce
1/2	cup reduced-fat or *fat-free sour cream (optional)
	baked tortilla chips

Layered Mexican Dip, Cont.

Process cheeses using #1 cone, onion using #2 cone.

Preheat electric skillet to 250 degrees, spray with vegetable spray. Add ground beef, when just barely pink add onion, cook until beef loses its pink color and onions are tender, drain. Stir refried beans into beef mixture. Spread mixture evenly in skillet. Layer green chiles over top of beef, spread 1/2 of cheese over this. Pour taco sauce over cheese. Sprinkle remaining cheese on top, cover, and bake at 250 degrees for 15 to 20 minutes.

Uncover, turn skillet to off, let cool for 5 to 10 minutes. Serve with sour cream and tortilla chips.

1 serving contains:

Cal	Prot	Fat	Carb	Fiber	Chol	Sodium
229	18.3 g	4.8 g	35 g	4.7 g	13.1 mg	686 mg

Strawberry Cream Cheese Jell-O Salad

Utensil: 2-quart saucepan
Yield: 10-15 servings

2	cups water
2	packages (0.3-ounces each) sugar-free strawberry gelatin
1	(8-ounce package)*fat-free cream cheese
1	(16-ounce) can crushed pineapple in own juice,drained, reserve juice
1	(12-ounce) container reduced-fat whipped topping
2	tablespoons chopped pecans

Put water in saucepan, bring to a boil. In a medium bowl dissolve gelatin in boiling water.

Drain pineapple, set aside. Add pineapple juice to gelatin. Cover and refrigerate until it just barely starts to gel.

Put cream cheese in large bowl, beat with electric mixer just to soften. Gradually add gelatin mixture to cheese, gently blend. Fold in crushed pineapple and whipped topping, gently blend. Pour into 9 X 13" pan. Sprinkle with chopped pecans. Cover and refrigerate until set.

1 serving contains:

Cal	Prot	Fat	Carb	Fiber	Chol	Sodium
115	4 g	6.4 g	11.7 g	0.4 g	2.7 mg	114 mg

Garden Vegetable Salad

Utensils: 3-quart saucepan, Steamer Inset, Saladmaster Machine
Yield: 6 servings

4	**cups water**
8	**medium potatoes**
2	**medium carrots**
2	**stalks broccoli**
1	**small zucchini**
$1/2$	**medium red onion**
$1/2$	**cup vinaigrette dressing of choice**

Process carrots using #2 cone, potatoes using #3 cone, zucchini, onion, and broccoli stalks using #4 cone.

Pour water in saucepan and bring to boil over medium heat. Place potatoes and cut broccoli stalks in steamer; insert in saucepan. Cover; steam 8 minutes or until tender. Meanwhile, place carrots in serving bowl. Cut broccoli heads into florets, add broccoli florets, zucchini, and onion to bowl.

When potatoes and broccoli stalks are tender, cool slightly and toss with vegetables and dressing. Serve salad at room temperature.

● ●

1 serving contains:

Cal	Prot	Fat	Carb	Fiber	Chol	Sodium
441	11.3 g	12.6 g	81.2 g	12.3 g	0 mg	225 mg

● ●

Green Bean Potato Salad: Omit carrots, broccoli, and zucchini. Substitute 4 cups cut green beans. Cook potatoes as in basic recipe above, adding beans after potatoes have steamed 5 minutes. Continue to steam an additional 10 minutes. Toss with thinly sliced red onion and dressing. Serve at room temperature. If salad will not be served promptly, run vegetables under cold water to stop cooking. Add dressing and toss before serving.

Mushrooms Florentine

Utensils: 2-quart saucepan, large skillet, Saladmaster Machine
Yield: 12 servings

1	ounce fresh Parmesan cheese
2	ounces reduced-fat or *fat-free cheddar cheese
1	tablespoon onion
2	teaspoons margarine
12	large mushrooms
1	clove garlic, minced
2	tablespoons chopped parsley
1/2	cup cooked, chopped spinach
1	teaspoon low-sodium soy sauce
	dash of grated nutmeg

Twist stems to remove from mushroom caps.
Process cheeses using #1 cone, onion and mushroom stems #2 cone.

Wipe caps and stems with a damp cloth. Place margarine in small saucepan; melt on medium heat, add chopped stems, grated onion, garlic, and parsley. Stir, cover; when Vapo-Valve clicks, reduce heat to low, and cook 2 minutes.

Remove lid; add spinach, soy sauce and cheddar cheese, stir until cheese is melted. Stuff a large spoonful of spinach mixture into each mushroom cap. Arrange caps in large skillet. Cover; place over medium heat, when Vapo-Valve clicks, reduce heat to low and cook 4-5 minutes. Dust tops with nutmeg and Parmesan cheese before serving.

Serve hot as appetizers, use to garnish meat dishes, or serve three per person as an entree.

• •

1 serving contains:

Cal	Prot	Fat	Carb	Fiber	Chol	Sodium
29.3	3.1 g	1.4 g	1.4 g	0.3 g	2.7 mg	108 mg

• •

Spicy Chicken Wings

Utensil: Large skillet
Yield: 8-10 servings

2	**pounds chicken winglets**
1	**teaspoon minced fresh or *^{1}/2 teaspoon ground ginger**
^{1}/2	**teaspoon minced garlic**
^{1}/3	**cup pineapple juice**
^{1}/4	**cup water**
^{1}/4	**cup reduced-sodium soy sauce**
^{1}/8	**teaspoon cayenne pepper**

If using whole wings, cut wings at both joints. Place winglets in large skillet, combine remaining ingredients for marinade and pour marinade over chicken. Cover; refrigerate 24 hours or more.

Drain off all but ^{1}/4 cup marinade. Cover; cook over medium heat until Vapo-Valve clicks. Reduce heat to low and cook 1 hour. Serve hot.

• •

1 serving contains:

Cal	Prot	Fat	Carb	Fiber	Chol	Sodium
249	21.3 g	15.3 g	4.9 g	0.1 g	63.5 mg	253 mg

• •

Easy hot wings: Cut wings as above, reserving pointy ends for other use. If using electric skillet, follow instructions for fried chicken. For stove-top preparation, preheat large skillet for 2 to 3 minutes over medium heat. Place wings, skin side down, in preheated skillet. Place cover slightly ajar on pan. Cook chicken 8 to 10 minutes or until evenly browned. Turn chicken, and place lid on pan. When Vapo-Valve clicks, reduce heat to low and cook chicken 15 minutes or until tender.

When chicken is cooked, pour over an entire bottle of Louisiana Hot Sauce, stirring to coat each piece evenly. Season with salt and pepper as desired. Replace cover on pan, again leaving slightly ajar and let chicken rest about 5 minutes before serving. Remove from pan to heated platter and serve "hot wings" with celery sticks and low-calorie Ranch dressing for dipping.

Dill-Marinated Shrimp

Utensil: 3-quart saucepan
Yield: 6 servings

Prepare a day or two in advance and marinate in the refrigerator to allow flavors to blend.

3/4	**pound medium shrimp**
1	**tablespoon water**
2	**lemon slices**
1	**bay leaf**
1	**cup rice wine vinegar**
1/4	**cup fresh dill, minced**
2	**scallions, thinly sliced**
1	**small celery stalk, thinly sliced**
	red leaf lettuce, garnish
	whole scallions, garnish
	lemon wedges, garnish

Peel and devein shrimp.

Place shrimp, water, lemon slices (lightly squeezed), and bay leaf in saucepan. Cover; cook over medium heat until Vapo-Valve clicks, reduce heat to low and cook 3 minutes. Remove lemon slices and bay leaf; cool to room temperature. Stir in vinegar, dill, sliced scallions, and celery; cover and refrigerate at least 24 hours, stirring once.

To serve, arrange on a lettuce-lined platter; garnish with whole scallions and lemon wedges.

• •

1 serving contains:

Cal	Prot	Fat	Carb	Fiber	Chol	Sodium
73.3	12.5 g	0.7 g	5 g	0.7 g	111 mg	36.8 mg

• •

VARIATIONS: Substitute 1/3 cup cider or white vinegar and 2/3 cup water for rice wine vinegar. One tablespoon dried dill can be substituted for fresh dill, but the dish will not be quite as tasty.

Bean Dip

Utensil: 3-quart saucepan
Yield 8-12 servings

1-1/2	cups cooked *pinto or kidney beans
1/2	cup broth from beans
1	medium tomato
1	small, fresh hot pepper
1	teaspoon cumin
1/4	teaspoon salt
1	clove garlic, minced
1/4	cup shredded sharp reduced-fat or *fat-free cheddar cheese
2	green onions, thinly sliced on diagonal
	tortilla chips or *baked tortilla chips

Place beans and bean broth in saucepan, mash. Put tomato, pepper, cumin, and salt in food processor or blender, process until smooth. Stir tomato mixture into beans and add garlic.

Cover, cook over medium heat, until Vapo-Valve clicks, reduce heat to low, cook 5 minutes. Remove from heat and allow to cool to room temperature. Stir, spoon into shallow serving bowl. Top with cheese in center and sliced green onions around the edge of the bowl. Serve with tortilla chips.

• •

1 serving contains:

Cal	Prot	Fat	Carb	Fiber	Chol	Sodium
51.6	3.8 g	0.3 g	8.9 g	2.9 g	0.8 mg	93.7 mg

• •

Shortcut: Drain and rinse 3 cans of pinto or kidney beans. Place beans in saucepan with enough chicken broth to moisten. Mash beans, adding a bit more broth if needed, to obtain desired consistency. Proceed with recipe.

No-fat corn chips

To make your own no-fat tortilla chips, begin with fresh corn tortillas. Cut them into quarters and place in a single layer on a baking sheet. Place in a 350-degree oven on bottom rack for about 15 minutes or until chips are crisp. For lower fat, more traditional chips, lightly brush tortilla pieces with a slight amount of oil or spray with vegetable spray and bake as above. If desired, while still warm, sprinkle with salt.

Eggplant Dip

Utensil: Large skillet
Yield: 15-20 servings

1	**large eggplant**
2	**cloves garlic**
1	**teaspoon water**
1/4	**cup olive oil**
1	**cup fresh parsley**
1/4	**cup walnuts**
2	**tablespoons lemon juice**

Cut eggplant in half lengthwise. Place unpeeled eggplant in large skillet, skin side down. Place one clove of garlic, without removing peel, in each eggplant half. Do not let garlic touch pan. Add 1 teaspoon water to bottom of pan. Cover; cook over medium heat until Vapo-Valve clicks, reduce heat to low and cook 30 minutes. Remove pan from heat and cool slightly.

Put garlic, oil, parsley, walnuts, and lemon juice in food processor or blender; process until smooth. Remove cooked garlic skin, scoop out eggplant pulp from the skin; add garlic and eggplant pulp to food processor, process until smooth.

Serve with pita bread cut into triangles.

1 serving contains:

Cal	Prot	Fat	Carb	Fiber	Chol	Sodium
41.1	0.7 g	3.6 g	2 g	1 g	0 mg	2.2 mg

Chicken Liver Pate

Utensil: Small skillet
Yield: 12-15 servings

1	**medium onion, chopped**
3/4	**pound chicken livers, halved**
1	**clove garlic, halved**
1/4	**teaspoon dried thyme**
1/4	**teaspoon freshly ground pepper**
	dash of salt
1	**boiled egg, finely chopped**
1	**tablespoon minced green onion (white only)**
1/4	**teaspoon freshly grated nutmeg**
1/4	**teaspoon sherry extract (optional)**

Place chopped onion in small skillet, spread chicken livers over onions in one layer. Add garlic, thyme, pepper, and salt. Cover; cook over medium heat until Vapo-Valve clicks, reduce heat to low and cook 8-10 minutes, or just until done. Remove from heat, uncover, and let livers cool slightly.

Set aside 3-4 livers; put remaining livers in a food processor or blender, process until smooth. Add onion and liquid from pan, barely mix. Remove pate from blender and place in bowl. Chop remaining livers, add to processed livers along with finely chopped egg.

Stir in minced scallions, nutmeg and extract. Cover and refrigerate several hours or overnight to blend flavors. Mound onto serving plate. Garnish with minced fresh parsley and serve with party rye bread or whole-grain crackers.

• •

1 serving contains:

Cal	Prot	Fat	Carb	Fiber	Chol	Sodium
43.9	6 g	1.6 g	1 g	0.1 g	157 mg	15.9 mg

• •

Party-Perfect Antipasto

Utensil: 3-quart saucepan
Yield: 8 servings

1	cup green beans
1/4	small head cauliflower
3	large stalks broccoli
12	asparagus spears
16	small mushrooms
2	slices onion
1	clove garlic, cut in half
1	cup cooked chick-peas or *kidney beans, drained
1	(6 1/2-ounce) can white albacore tuna in water, drained
16	black olives
2	cups cubed reduced-fat or *fat-free mozzarella cheese

Marinade

1/2	cup olive oil
3	tablespoons red wine vinegar
1/2	teaspoon dried oregano
1/4	teaspoon mustard powder
1/8	teaspoon salt
1/8	teaspoon freshly ground pepper
1/8	teaspoon paprika

Party-Perfect Antipasto, Cont.

Leave green beans whole; remove stem ends. Break cauliflower into florets. Trim florets from stalks (save stalks for soup), separate broccoli into florets. Snap tough ends from asparagus. Clean mushrooms by removing any loose soil; trim stems.

Rinse beans, cauliflower, broccoli, asparagus, and mushrooms place in saucepan. Cover; cook over medium heat until Vapo-Valve clicks, reduce heat to low and cook 3-4 minutes, until vegetables are crisp-tender. (They will continue to cook slightly while marinating.)

While vegetables are cooking, combine all marinade ingredients in a small bowl. Pour 1/3 of the marinade, with 1 onion slice and 1/2 clove garlic, over chick-peas; cover and refrigerate.

Without draining liquids from vegetables, add remaining marinade, onion slice, and 1/2 clove garlic. Cover and refrigerate to chill before serving.

To serve, remove top of tuna can and drain well. Open bottom of tuna can; invert over a round platter, and push tuna through can in one piece. Arrange vegetables, chick-peas, olives, and cheese on the platter around the tuna, grouping the individual vegetables and creating a colorful design.

1 serving contains:

Cal	Prot	Fat	Carb	Fiber	Chol	Sodium
269	21.5 g	15.2 g	14.5 g	5.6 g	18 mg	419 mg

Tomato Salsa

Tomato Salsa isn't just for dipping, its taste is so well-liked we've found ways to include it in a variety of recipes. Enjoy!

Utensil: 1-quart saucepan
Yield: 4 1/2-5 cups

1	**clove garlic, halved**
1	**hot red chili pepper, halved and seeded**
1	**medium onion, quartered**
6	**cups quartered tomatoes (about 4-5 whole)**
2	**tablespoons minced, fresh coriander leaves**
	tortilla chips

Place garlic, pepper, and onion in food processeor or blender, add ¹/₂ cup of tomatoes. Process slightly, leave a little chunky, add remaining tomatoes, process just slightly to combined, place in saucepan. Cover; cook over medium heat until Vapo-Valve clicks, reduce heat to low and cook 2 minutes. Remove from heat, stir in coriander. Allow to cool before serving with tortilla chips.

1 serving contains:

Cal	Prot	Fat	Carb	Fiber	Chol	Sodium
24.4	0.9 g	0.3 g	5.5 g	1.4 g	0 mg	6.6 mg

Stuffed Tiny Red Potatoes

Utensil: 3-quart saucepan
Yield: 12-24 servings

24	**tiny new red potatoes**
¹/₃	**cup plain, *reduced-fat or fat-free yogurt**
¹/₄	**cup reduced fat or *fat-free sour cream**
2	**tablespoons fresh chives, minced**
	dash of freshly ground black pepper
24	**2-inch pieces of fresh chives, garnish**
	parsley, garnish

Select small potatoes, about "two-bite" size. Scrub potatoes; do not peel, place in saucepan. Cover; cook over medium heat until Vapo-Valve clicks, reduce heat to low and cook about 15-18 minutes or until tender. Cool to room temperature.

Place potatoes on work surface so they lay flat, using a knife, partially hollow out the top of each potato. Just before serving, combine yogurt, sour cream, chives, and black pepper, place a small spoonful of mixture in each potato. To garnish, tie each chive in a loose knot and place atop the yogurt and sour cream mixture. Arrange parsley on serving platter, then place potatoes on bed of parsley.

1 serving contains:

Cal	Prot	Fat	Carb	Fiber	Chol	Sodium
73.6	2.4 g	0.05 g	15.4 g	0.01 g	0.2 mg	234 mg

Party Pasta Salad

Utensils: Dutch oven, 3-quart saucepan, Steamer Inset, Saladmaster Machine
Yield: 8 servings

4	**cups pasta (radiatore, fusili, spirals, or combination)**
2	**small carrots**
2	**celery stalks**
1	**onion**
1	**cup broccoli florets**
1	**tablespoon fresh basil or *parsley minced**
3/4	**cup choice of vinaigrette dressing**

Process carrots, celery and onion using #4 cone.

Place 3 quarts water in Dutch oven and bring to boil over medium heat, covered. Lightly salt water and stir in pasta. Return water to boil and cook 6-8 minutes, just until firm-tender. Drain into colander, rinse under cold running water, drain again. Set aside.

Place water in saucepan, bring to a boil over medium heat. Place carrots, celery, onion, and broccoli in steamer inset. Cover; steam 2-3 minutes, or until vegetables are crisp-tender. Place steamer inset under cold running water until vegetables are cooled. Drain well.

Place pasta and vegetables in large serving bowl. Add fresh basil or parsley and dressing. Toss and serve, or refrigerate to chill.

• •

1 serving contains:

Cal	Prot	Fat	Carb	Fiber	Chol	Sodium
314	7.6 g	14.2 g	45.1 g	3.5 g	0 mg	196 mg

• •

Hot Linguini Salad: Use 1/2 pound regular linguini and 1/2 pound spinach linguini, cook as in Party Pasta Salad, but do not rinse. Omit celery, onion, and broccoli. Cut carrots in julienne strips; steam 2 minutes. Add 1 zucchini, cut in julienne strips, and 1 cup peas, and steam an additional 2 minutes. When pasta is done, toss with steamed vegetables, basil or parsley, and vinaigrette. Serve hot.

Potato Salad

Utensils: 3-quart saucepan, Steamer Inset
Yield: 10 servings

4	**cups water**
4	**medium potatoes**
2	**tablespoons lemon juice**
1	**teaspoon fresh dill weed, minced**
1	**medium cucumber, diced**
1	**medium green pepper, diced**
1	**medium tomato, diced**
1/2	**cup *reduced-fat or fat-free, creamy Italian dressing**

Pour water into saucepan; bring to boil over medium heat. Place potatoes in steamer inset; place over boiling water. Cover; steam 15 minutes or until potatoes are tender. Remove potatoes, set aside to cool. When cool, peel and dice; place in a medium bowl. Add lemon juice, dill, cucumber, pepper and tomato. Add dressing; toss gently, cover, and chill.

1 serving contains:

Cal	Prot	Fat	Carb	Fiber	Chol	Sodium
109	2.2 g	0.7 g	22.8 g	2.5 g	0.7 mg	103 mg

Other dressings

- 1/4 cup reduced-fat mayonnaise, 3 tablespoons Dijon mustard and 1/4 cup plain yogurt

- 1/2 cup nonfat bottled ranch-style dressing (omit dill and add 2 to 3 sliced green onions, including green part)

- 1/2 cup nonfat bottled Catalina dressing (omit dill and add 1 small can mandarin orange slices, drained)

Continental Vegetable Salad

Utensils: Large skillet, Saladmaster Machine
Yield: 8 servings

3	medium carrots
2	cups fresh green beans, approx. 1 pound
2	cups cauliflower florets
1	small red or green pepper, seeded and cut into strips
1	medium yellow squash
1/4	cup olive oil
1/4	cup rice wine vinegar
1	tablespoon lemon juice
1	teaspoon Dijon-style mustard
1/4	teaspoon dried oregano
1/4	teaspoon dried marjoram
1/2	clove garlic, minced

Process carrots and squash using #4 cone.

Trim ends of green beans and place in large skillet. Cover; cook over medium heat until Vapo-Valve clicks, reduce heat to low and cook 2 minutes.

Add carrots to pan quickly, cover; cook an additional 2 minutes. Add cauliflower, pepper, and squash, cook an additional 4-5 minutes or until all vegetables are just crisp-tender.

While vegetables are cooking, combine ingredients for dressing. Pour dressing over cooked vegetables. Serve hot.

To serve the salad chilled, run cold water over the vegetables after cooking to cool them. Add dressing, toss, and refrigerate until chilled.

1 serving contains:

Cal	Prot	Fat	Carb	Fiber	Chol	Sodium
104	2 g	7.2 g	10 g	3.3 g	0 mg	32.5 mg

Gourmet garnish

Caviar in a jar is a relatively inexpensive way to add a gourmet look and flavor to a special hors d'oeuvre. Purchase red, black or golden caviar (or combine them for additional color) and lightly sprinkle on top of potatoes, omitting the chives. For a pretty plate, serve some with the chive garnish, others with the caviar.

Cream of Chicken Soup
with Vegetables

Soups and Stews

Few dishes are more rewarding nutritionally or flavor-wise than soups. The original one-dish meal, soups are an aid to those watching their caloric intake. Provided that the soup is not cream-based or filled with too many rich ingredients, it can be a low-calorie beginning to a meal. As such it can satisfy an appetite before the rest of the meal, easing temptation to eat larger portions.

Because soup is a hot dish that invites slow sipping, a bowl of brothy soup before a meal takes time to eat. Thus your brain has time to get that "satisfied" feeling from the stomach.

A large bowl of a healthful, nutritious soup like our Low Cholesterol Chicken and Lime Soup or Hearty Low-Calorie Lentil Soup with a garden salad can be a filling lunch or light supper.

Flavors are rich, textures are mouth-filling and, often, the ingredients are economical. Soups are perfect solutions to busy lifestyles. They hold well and store and reheat with ease, actually improving in flavor quite often. And a dish like vegetable soup makes using bits of leftovers or vegetable and meat trimmings an appetizing way to get the most from your food dollar.

This chapter is full of techniques that will show you how to make soups taste as if they were rich with cream without the addition of rich ingredients. Using low-fat or skim milk or vegetable purees to thicken soups and sauces is the contemporary way to enjoy flavor and texture without fat.

Because they are as varied as the ingredients you have on hand and are easily prepared, soups and stews are adaptable to the dietary and taste preferences of any palate.

Low Cholesterol Chicken and Lime Soup

It seems like an unusual pairing, but we have found the brisk, tart flavor of lime adds a subtle flavor to the chicken.

Utensils: Large skillet, 7-quart Dutch oven, Saladmaster Machine
Yield: 5 servings

1	**fresh lime**
1	**medium onion**
4	**boneless chicken breast halves, skinned**
2	**6" flour tortillas**
6	**cups low-fat, low-sodium chicken broth**
1	**(4-ounce) can mild green chilies, chopped**
1/2	**teaspoon dried oregano**
1/8	**teaspoon black pepper**
1	**clove garlic, minced**
1	**cup tomato, chopped**
2	**tablespoons *parsley or cilantro, snipped**

Shred lime peel using #1 cone, squeeze juice from lime and set aside. Process onion using #2 cone.

Cut chicken breasts into bite-size pieces, set aside. Cut each tortilla into 5 wedges. Preheat skillet on medium heat. Place tortillas in skillet; toast 8-10 minutes or until light brown. Remove from skillet; cool.

In Dutch oven combine chicken broth, onion, chilies, oregano, 1/4 teaspoon lime peel, 2 tablespoons lime juice, black pepper and garlic. Bring to boil. Reduce heat to low; simmer 5 minutes. Stir in chicken, cover; cook over medium heat until Vapo-Valve clicks, reduce heat to low and cook 7-9 minutes or until chicken is tender. Stir in tomato; heat thoroughly.

When ready to serve sprinkle with parsley or cilantro. Serve with tortilla wedges.

• •

1 serving contains:

Cal	Prot	Fat	Carb	Fiber	Chol	Sodium
323	48.1 g	6.3 g	16.2 g	1.8 g	118 mg	226 mg

• •

Creamy Spinach Soup

Utensils: 2-quart saucepan, Saladmaster Machine
Yield: 6 servings

1	**large carrot**
$^1/_2$	**medium onion**
2	**tablespoons margarine**
2	**tablespoons flour**
1	**teaspoon salt or seasoning *substitute**
$^1/_2$	**teaspoon dry mustard**
1	**(14-14 $^1/_2$-ounce) can low-fat, low-sodium chicken broth**
1	**(10-ounce) package frozen chopped spinach**
2 $^1/_2$	**cups 2% milk**
1	**tablespoon fresh lemon juice**

Process carrot using #1 cone, onion using #2 cone.

Place margarine in saucepan; melt at low heat. Blend in flour, salt, and mustard. Remove from heat; stir in chicken broth. Heat to boil over medium heat; stir constantly. Add spinach, carrot and onion. Cover; when Vapo-Valve clicks, reduce heat to low and cook 5-6 minutes or until spinach is thawed and vegetables are tender. Return heat to medium-low, stir in milk and lemon juice, cook 2-3 minutes or until hot.

• •

1 serving contains:

Cal	Prot	Fat	Carb	Fiber	Chol	Sodium
122	6.2 g	6 g	11.6 g	1.8 g	9.4 mg	163 mg

• •

Thicken without fat

Instant dissolving flour is a real plus for thickening without added fat. Dissolve 2 tablespoons instant dissolving flour in $^1/_4$ cup liquid, water, broth, milk or cooking liquid. Stir into soup to thicken. If additional thickening is desired, shake flour into soup kettle and stir to dissolve.

Crab Gumbo

Utensil: 3-quart saucepan
Yield: 4 servings

1	teaspoon canola oil
1/2	cup green pepper, chopped
1/2	cup green onion, sliced
1	clove garlic, minced
3	cups low-fat, low-sodium chicken broth
2	medium tomatoes, peeled and chopped
1/8	teaspoon celery powder
1/8	teaspoon dried thyme, crushed
1/8	teaspoon hot pepper sauce
1	cup frozen sliced okra
1	(6-ounce) can crabmeat
1/2	cup turkey ham diced
2	cups hot cooked rice

Pour oil in saucepan; heat on medium heat. Add green pepper, onion and garlic, sauté until vegetables are tender. Stir in chicken broth, tomatoes, celery powder, thyme and pepper sauce, bring to boil over medium heat. Stir in okra, cover; when Vapo-Valve clicks reduce heat to low and cook 10 minutes or until okra is tender.

Drain, flake and remove cartilage from crabmeat. Stir crabmeat and turkey ham into gumbo. Heat thoroughly on medium. Serve over rice in soup bowl.

● ●

1 serving contains:

Cal	Prot	Fat	Carb	Fiber	Chol	Sodium
283	20.8 g	3.9 g	40.6 g	2.9 g	54.3 mg	470 mg

● ●

Presto orzo: Gumbo also spoons well over rice-shaped pasta called orzo. It cooks in about half the time of rice. Simply bring a pot of water to a boil, cook according to package directions, drain and use as rice with gumbo.

Turkey-Vegetable Chili

Utensil: 3-quart saucepan, Saladmaster Machine
Yield: 6 servings

1/2	**medium green pepper**
1/4	**small onion**
2	**small zucchini**
1	**teaspoon olive oil**
2	**cloves garlic, minced**
3	**cups cooked *turkey or chicken, diced**
1/2	**cup water**
1	**tablespoon dried oregano**
1	**tablespoon chili powder**
1	**teaspoon ground cumin**
1	**cup fresh whole tomatoes, cooked and crushed**
1	**(10-ounce) package frozen mixed vegetables**

Process pepper and onion on #2 cone, zucchini on #4 cone, (cover and refrigerate zucchini).

Heat oil in saucepan over medium heat. Add green pepper, onion and garlic; sauté 3 minutes stirring frequently. Add remaining ingredients except frozen vegetables and zucchini. Cover; when Vapo-Valve clicks, reduce heat to low and cook 1 hour, stirring occasionally. Stir in frozen vegetables and zucchini; bring to a boil over medium heat. Reduce heat to low, and simmer uncovered 5 minutes until zucchini is tender.

● ●

1 serving contains:

Cal	Prot	Fat	Carb	Fiber	Chol	Sodium
206	27.1 g	5 g	14.7 g	4.5 g	37.4 mg	809 mg

● ●

Vegetarian chili

For meatless chili, substitute navy or cannelloni beans for the turkey or chicken. Simply rinse and drain 3 cans of beans. Add to soup as directed for turkey or chicken.

Simple Chili

There's nothing like a basic chili for a cold winter day or brisk summer evening. A bonus: Save the leftovers, chili just gets better.

Utensils: 7-quart Dutch oven, Saladmaster Machine
Yield: 6 servings

1	large onion
2	pounds chili meat or *ground beef or ground turkey
1	clove garlic, minced
1	teaspoon salt or seasoning *substitute
1\2	teaspoon freshly ground black pepper (more if desired)
1\4	teaspoon cayenne pepper (more if desired)
1	tablespoon chili powder (more if desired)
1/2	teaspoon basil
1/2	teaspoon savory
3	bay leaves
1	(14-ounce) can tomato sauce
1	(14-ounce) can peeled whole tomatoes
1	cup water

Process onion using #2 cone.

Preheat Dutch oven on medium heat; add chili meat, brown, drain fat. Add onion and garlic, cook until onion is tender; add remaining ingredients. Cover; when Vapo-Valve clicks, reduce heat to low and cook 1 hour.

1 serving contains:

Cal	Prot	Fat	Carb	Fiber	Chol	Sodium
456	39.3 g	29 g	10.6 g	2.3 g	132 mg	633 mg

Sweet Potato Bisque

Utensils: 3-quart saucepan, Saladmaster Machine
Yield: 6 servings

2	celery stalks
1	large, tart apple, cored
2-3	sweet potatoes, peeled (about 1 1/2 pounds)
1/4	cup shallots or *scallions, white part only, chopped
2	cups 2% milk or *skim milk
1	cup low-fat, low-sodium chicken broth

2 **tablespoons sherry or Madeira wine (optional)**
1/8 **teaspoon ground allspice**
6 **tablespoons plain, *reduced-fat or fat-free yogurt**
1 **tablespoon fresh parsley, minced**

Process celery and apple using #2 cone, potatoes using #3 cone.
Place potatoes, celery, apple, and shallots in saucepan. Add milk, broth, sherry (if desired), and allspice. Cover; cook over medium heat until Vapo-Valve clicks, reduce heat to low, and cook 20-25 minutes, or until potatoes are quite soft.

 Put cooked vegetables and apple in a food processor or blender, process until smooth. Return to pan with liquids, thin if necessary with additional broth or milk. (For special occasions, when a richer soup may be desired, add 1/2 cup light cream.) Serve hot, topped with a dollop of yogurt and sprinkled with parsley.

1 serving contains:

Cal	Prot	Fat	Carb	Fiber	Chol	Sodium
179	6.2 g	0.6 g	37.8 g	4.3 g	2.3 mg	85.6 mg

Chicken Vegetable Soup

Utensils: 7-quart Dutch oven, 11-inch lid, Saladmaster Machine
Yield: 6 servings

3 **celery stalks**
2 **leeks (white part only)**
1 **large onion**
4 **small carrots**
8 **cups low-fat, low-sodium chicken broth**
1/2 **cup *dry white wine or additional stock**
1 **bay leaf**
1 **clove garlic, minced**
1 **teaspoon ground sage**
1 **teaspoon leaf thyme**
2 **boneless chicken breast halves, skinned**
1/2 **teaspoon salt**
 dash of freshly ground pepper

Chicken Vegetable Soup, Cont.

Process celery, leeks, onion and carrots using #2 cone.

Place chicken broth, wine, bay leaf, garlic, sage, thyme and chicken in Dutch oven. Cover; cook over medium heat until Vapo-Valve clicks, reduce heat to low, and cook about 15-20 minutes or until chicken is tender.

Remove chicken breast halves from soup, add celery, leeks, onion and carrots. Cover; return to medium heat. When Vapo-Valve clicks, reduce heat to low and cook 10-15 minutes, or until tender. While vegetables are cooking, cut chicken breasts into strips, stir into finished soup. Season with salt and pepper. Remove bay leaf before serving.

● ●

1 serving contains:

Cal	Prot	Fat	Carb	Fiber	Chol	Sodium
171	22.4 g	2.3 g	10.1 g	2.4 g	49.7 mg	329 mg

● ●

Chicken soup variations: Add 1 1/2 teaspoons minced fresh tarragon with vegetables in basic recipe. *Chicken Corn Soup:* Substitute 1 1/2 cups frozen corn kernels in place of peas in the creamed variation that follows. *Cream of Chicken Soup with Vegetables:* Dice vegetables and add 1/4 cup diced sweet red pepper. Cook soup as in basic recipe above, dicing chicken instead of cutting into strips. Blend 2 cups soft-cooked rice with 1/2 cup of the chicken stock until smooth. Stir into soup. Add 1 cup peas. Cover; cook over medium heat until Vapo-Valve clicks and peas are just tender. Remove from heat and serve.

Fish Chowder

Utensils: 3-quart saucepan, Saladmaster Machine
Yield: 4 servings

Use any firm white fish—flounder, pollock, hake, halibut, perch, red snapper, bass, or tilefish—in place of haddock.

3-4	**medium red potatoes**
1/4	**medium onion**
3 1/2	**cups low-fat, low-sodium fish or *chicken broth**
1	**cup tomatoes, chopped and seeded**
1	**teaspoon garlic, minced**
1	**tablespoon fresh lemon juice**
1/4	**teaspoon dried thyme**

1   bay leaf
3/4   pound haddock fillets, cut into bite-size pieces
1/4   cup green onions, thinly sliced
2   tablespoons fresh parsley, minced
     thinly sliced lemon, garnish

Process potatoes using #3 cone, onions using #2 cone.

Place potatoes, onion, broth, tomatoes, garlic, lemon juice, thyme, and bay leaf in saucepan. Cover; cook over medium heat until Vapo-Valve clicks. Reduce heat to low and cook 15 minutes.

Stir in fish and green onions, cook over low heat, covered, an additional 5 minutes. Remove bay leaf, stir in parsley, garnish with lemon slices, and serve hot.

1 serving contains:

Cal	Prot	Fat	Carb	Fiber	Chol	Sodium
209	27.9 g	1 g	63.7 g	1.1 g	63.7 mg	359 mg

Creamy Corn Soup with Crabmeat

Utensil: 2-quart saucepan
Yield: 8 servings

3 1/2 cups low-fat, low-sodium chicken broth
1 1/2 cups *fresh or frozen corn kernels
2   1/4-inch slices fresh gingerroot, peeled
1   tablespoon sake (optional)
1/2   teaspoon sugar
1/4   teaspoon salt
      dash of freshly ground black pepper
2   tablespoons cornstarch
1/4   cup water
2   (3-ounce) cans flaked crabmeat
1   egg white, slightly beaten
2   green onions, thinly sliced

Place chicken broth, corn, and ginger in saucepan. Cover; cook over medium heat until Vapo-Valve clicks, reduce heat to low, and cook 5 minutes.

Creamy Corn Soup with Crabmeat, Cont.

Discard ginger slices. Strain hot stock mixture into medium bowl. Puree corn in blender or food processor with $1/2$ cup stock until smooth. Press corn puree through fine sieve, using back of wooden spoon. Discard remaining corn pulp in strainer.

Return corn and stock mixture to saucepan over medium heat and stir in sake (if desired), sugar, salt, and pepper. In small bowl, combine cornstarch and water. When soup begins to boil; stir in cornstarch mixture, stir for 1 minute while soup thickens.

Reduce heat to low, stir in crabmeat. Remove pan from heat. Slowly add beaten egg white, stirring constantly in circular motion; add green onions.

1 serving contains:

Cal	Prot	Fat	Carb	Fiber	Chol	Sodium
74.1	7.1 g	0.7 g	10.4 g	1.7 g	19.2 mg	174 mg

Beef Stew

Utensils: 7-quart Dutch oven, Saladmaster Machine
Yield: 10-12 servings

1	medium onion
6	medium potatoes
2	large leeks
8	medium carrots
1	pound lean beef, cubed
8	cups water
2	cups tomato sauce
2	bay leaves
3	celery stalks, cut into 1" pieces
2	cups fresh pearl onions (about $1/2$ pound)
1	cup mushrooms, quartered
$2/3$	cup tomato paste
6	cloves garlic, minced
$1/2$	teaspoon dried basil
$1/2$	teaspoon dried marjoram
$1/2$	teaspoon dried oregano
$1/4$	teaspoon dried thyme
$1/4$	cup fresh chives or parsley, minced

Process onion using #2 cone, potatoes using #3 cone, leeks using #4 cone, carrots using #5 cone.

Preheat Dutch oven 2-3 minutes over medium heat. Pat beef cubes dry with paper towel, place in Dutch oven and brown on all sides, stir in onion, cook 2-3 minutes. Add water, scraping browned particles of meat from bottom of pan with a wooden spoon and stirring into liquid. Stir in tomato sauce and bay leaves. Cover; when Vapo-Valve clicks, reduce heat to low, and cook 1-1 $1/2$ hours.

Remove bay leaves; add celery, pearl onions, mushrooms, potatoes, leeks, carrots, tomato paste, garlic, basil, marjoram, oregano, and thyme, stir. Cover; return heat to medium. When Vapo-Valve clicks, reduce heat to low and cook 45 minutes to 1 hour. Remove bay leaf, stir in minced fresh chives or parsley just before serving.

● ●

1 serving contains:

Cal	Prot	Fat	Carb	Fiber	Chol	Sodium
232	12.6 g	12 g	20.1 g	3.8 g	38.7 mg	413 mg

● ●

French Onion Soup

Utensils: 7-quart Dutch oven, Saladmaster Machine;
Yield: 4 servings

2	large sweet Spanish onions
2	teaspoons olive oil
1	tablespoon whole wheat flour
1	clove garlic, minced
4	cups low-fat, low-sodium chicken broth
2	tablespoons reduced-sodium soy sauce
$1/2$	teaspoon dark molasses
	croutons (garnish)
	minced fresh parsley (garnish)

Cut onions in half lengthwise, process using #4 cone. Heat oil in Dutch oven over medium heat, add onions, stir frequently until lightly browned.

When onions are tender and begin to turn golden brown, sprinkle on flour; stir until onions are coated. Add garlic, broth, soy sauce, and molasses. Cover; when Vapo-Valve clicks reduce heat to low, and cook 15-20 minutes. Serve garnished with croutons and minced parsley.

French Onion Soup, Cont.

● ●

1 serving contains:

Cal	Prot	Fat	Carb	Fiber	Chol	Sodium
120	5.6 g	2.6 g	18.7 g	3 g	0.8 mg	300 mg

● ●

Lentil Soup

The ever-reliable English soup has been a favorite in European countries for decades. Its popularity stems from the lentils' mellow taste, which may be complimented by a variety of seasonings.

Utensils: 3-quart saucepan, Saladmaster Machine
Yield: 6 servings

1	**large carrot**
2	**celery stalks, divided**
1/3	**medium onion**
1 1/2	**cups lentils**
6	**cups water**
2	**cloves garlic**
3	**whole cloves**
1/8	**teaspoon dried thyme**
6	**thin lemon slices**

Process onion using #2 cone, 1 celery stalk and carrot #4 cone.

Place lentils and water in saucepan. Peel one garlic clove and stick whole cloves into the garlic, add to lentils. Cover; cook over medium heat until Vapo-Valve clicks, reduce heat to low and cook 45 minutes.

Discard garlic clove stuck with cloves. Mince remaining garlic clove and add to lentils along with carrot, remaining celery, onion, and thyme. Cover; cook over medium heat until valve clicks, reduce heat to low, and cook an additional 20 minutes. Add lemon slices, cover and remove from heat. Let stand 5 minutes, stir, and serve.

● ●

1 serving contains:

Cal	Prot	Fat	Carb	Fiber	Chol	Sodium
84	5.3 g	0.4 g	16.1 g	4.2 g	0 mg	42.8 mg

● ●

Split Pea Soup

Utensil: 7-quart Dutch oven, Saladmaster Machine
Yield: 8 servings

2	**cups dried split peas**
8	**cups water**
1	**bay leaf**
1	**leek**
1	**medium sweet Spanish onion**
3	**celery stalks**
2	**medium potatoes**
1	**ham bone or *1/2 pound smoked turkey in chunks**
1/4	**cup minced fresh parsley**
1/2	**teaspoon salt**
	dash of freshly ground pepper
	dash of fresh lemon juice

Place split peas and water in Dutch oven. Cover; cook over medium heat until Vapo-Valve clicks, reduce heat to low, and cook 45 minutes. While peas are cooking; process leek, onion and celery using #2 cone, potatoes #3 cone.

Add vegetables and ham bone, stir. Cover; cook over medium heat until valve clicks again, stir, reduce heat to low and cook 30 minutes.

Remove bay leaf and ham bone. Stir in parsley, salt, and pepper. Put in a food processor or blender, process until smooth. Return to Dutch oven to keep warm. Flavor with a dash of lemon juice before serving.

● ●

1 serving contains:

Cal	Prot	Fat	Carb	Fiber	Chol	Sodium
230	18.8 g	1.7 g	36.5 g	7.8 g	10.8 mg	429 mg

● ●

Split Pea Soup Deluxe: After soup is pureed, add 2 cups fresh or frozen peas, 1/4 cup light cream, and 2 or 3 minced fresh basil leaves to soup (or 1/4 teaspoon dried basil). Return to medium heat, cover; when Vapo-Valve clicks, reduce heat to low, and cook just 1-2 minutes until peas are tender. Serve hot.

Vegetable Bean Soup with Ham

Utensils: 7-quart Dutch oven, Saladmaster Machine
Yield: 5 servings

3/4	cup dry navy beans
5	cups water, divided
1	medium onion
2	medium carrots
1	celery stalk
2	cups fresh spinach or *cabbage
3	cups low-sodium broth
1	teaspoon dried basil
1/2	teaspoon dried thyme
1/4	teaspoon freshly ground black pepper
2	bay leaves
1	clove garlic, minced
1 1/2	cups diced, cooked ham or *1/2 pound smoked turkey in chunks

Rinse beans, place in Dutch oven add 4 cups of water. Bring to a boil over medium heat, reduce heat to low; simmer 2 minutes, remove from heat. Cover; let stand 1 hour.

While beans are softening, process onion using #2 cone, carrots and celery using #4 cone, spinach or cabbage #5 cone.

Drain and rinse beans, return to Dutch oven, add 5 cups water, carrots, onion, celery, bouillon cubes, basil, thyme, pepper, bay leaves and garlic. Bring to a boil over medium heat; reduce heat to low. Cover; simmer 1-2 hours or until beans are tender. Stir in ham and spinach or cabbage; simmer 3-5 minutes. Remove bay leaves.

● ●

1 serving contains:

Cal	Prot	Fat	Carb	Fiber	Chol	Sodium
143	15 g	2.1 g	16.6 g	4.7 g	21.4 mg	399 mg

● ●

Hearty Low-Calorie Lentil Stew

Utensils: 7-quart Dutch oven, Large skillet, Saladmaster Machine;
Yield: 8 servings

1	medium onion
2	celery stalks
1	cup dried lentils, rinsed and sorted
4	cups low-fat, low-sodium beef broth or *water
2	cloves garlic, minced
2	(16-ounce) cans low-sodium tomatoes, chopped
1	teaspoon dried rosemary, crumbled
1/4	teaspoon black pepper
4	medium carrots, peeled and cut into 1-inch lengths, divided
1	tablespoon margarine
8	small white pearl onions, peeled
1/4	pound small mushrooms, halved
4	medium potatoes, peeled and cut into 1-inch cubes

Process onion and celery using #2 cone.

In the Dutch oven combine onion, celery, lentils, beef broth, garlic, tomatoes, rosemary, pepper, and half the carrots. Cover; cook over medium heat until the Vapo-Valve clicks. Reduce heat to low and cook for 35 minutes.

Melt margarine in skillet over medium heat, add remaining carrots and pearl onions; cook for 5-8 minutes or until lightly browned. Add mushrooms, continue to cook, stirring frequently, for 2 to 3 minutes.

Add potatoes and the skillet vegetables to the Dutch oven, cover; when Vapo-Valve clicks reduce heat to low and cook 20-25 minutes or until the lentils and potatoes are tender. Serve with white or brown rice if desired.

1 serving contains:

Cal	Prot	Fat	Carb	Fiber	Chol	Sodium
225	11 g	2.5 g	43.3 g	8.4 g	0 mg	58.8 mg

Healthy Vegetable Stew

Utensils: 7-quart Dutch oven, Saladmaster Machine
Yield: 4 servings

2	**large yellow onions**
2	**large stalks celery**
1	**medium yellow squash**
1	**teaspoon olive oil**
2	**cloves garlic, minced**
1	**(16-ounce) can low-sodium tomatoes, chopped**
1	**cup *fresh or frozen lima beans**
1/2	**cup dry white wine or *low-fat, low-sodium chicken broth**
1	**bay leaf**
3/4	**teaspoon dried thyme**
3/4	**teaspoon basil**
3/4	**teaspoon marjoram**
1/4	**teaspoon black pepper**
1/8	**teaspoon cayenne pepper**
2	**cups cooked and drained white beans**
1	**teaspoon lemon juice**
2	**tablespoons parsley, minced**

Process onion and celery using #2 cone, squash using #4 cone.

Heat olive oil in Dutch oven over medium heat; add onions, celery and garlic. Cook uncovered about 5-8 minutes or until onion and celery are soft. Add squash, tomatoes, lima beans, wine, bay leaf, thyme, basil, marjoram, black pepper, and cayenne pepper. Cover; cook until Vapo-Valve clicks, reduce heat to low, and cook for 10 minutes.

Add white beans, stir, simmer 5 minutes. Stir in the lemon juice and parsley before serving.

● ●

1 serving contains:

Cal	Prot	Fat	Carb	Fiber	Chol	Sodium
418	23 g	3.1 g	80.2 g	27.1 g	0.1 mg	71.1 mg

● ●

Spiced Green Beans
with Peanuts

Vegetables

Five-a-day, that's all it takes for good vegetable and fruit nutrition. The good news is that with imaginative cooking and a variety of fresh vegetables for side dishes and salads, it is surprisingly easy to get the recommended number of daily servings.

The real bonus with the Saladmaster cooking system is that the techniques allow the cook to preserve as many of the nutrients as possible. You don't pour vitamins down the drain with cooking water. And the waterless system maximizes the natural flavor of the produce so you don't have to add a lot of butter, salt, sugar or other seasonings.

Concentrate on produce that is high in the cancer-fighting antioxidant vitamins—C, A and E. Red, yellow, and green leafy vegetables are at the top of this list. Of course, vegetables offer other advantages as well. They are high in fiber which can promote heart health as well as fitness of the digestive tract. Among the best for those benefits are the cruciferous vegetables—the cabbage family, including broccoli.

Whenever possible choose fresh vegetables and select those in season for the best nutritional and economic value. Frozen vegetables are next best when it comes to nutrition. Although convenient, canned vegetables lack the tender-crisp texture of lightly cooked fresh or frozen vegetables. To maximize ease of vegetable preparation, refer to the guidelines for cooking times.

Cooking vegetables the Saladmaster way

Remember that pans should be at least $^2/_3$-full. Avoid peeling vegetables, whenever possible, since much of the vitamins and nutrients are in the skins.

Follow this simple two-step process:

1. Place fresh vegetables in correct size pan. Add enough water to pan to cover vegetables. Shake pan and drain. This restores water lost by the vegetables during shipping and storage. When using frozen vegetables, simply place in pan; do not rinse.

2. Cover pan with lid and place pan over medium heat. When Vapo-Valve clicks, reduce heat to low. Begin timing vegetables according to the chart below.

Vegetable	Minutes
Asparagus, whole spears	5-7
Beans, green or wax	8-10
Beets, red, whole medium	50-60
Broccoli spears	5-7
Brussels sprouts	9-10
Cabbage, sliced	4-6
Carrots, sliced	9-10
Cauliflower, separated	6-8
Celery, sliced	5-7
Corn, kernels, frozen	1-2
Corn on the cob	10-12
Okra, small, whole	6-8
Onions, sliced	8-10
Peas, fresh or frozen	2-3
Peppers, green or red	3-4
Potatoes, sweet, cubed	15-20
Potatoes, white, whole, medium	20-25
Snow peas	2-3
Spinach, fresh	2-3
Squash, summer, sliced	4-6
Squash, winter, diced	10-13
Zucchini squash, sliced	4-6

Note: *For crisp-tender vegetables, rely on briefest times shown. If you prefer more tender vegetables, cook according to longer times. Frozen vegetables are usually better when cooked the shorter times. For use in casseroles, vegetables should be undercooked so they don't get too soft when combined with other ingredients for final cooking.*

Waldorf Rice

Utensils: Large skillet, Saladmaster Machine
Yield: 6-8 servings

2	celery stalks
1/2	cup toasted almonds
1	large apple, cored
3/4	cup brown rice
1 1/2	cups unsweetened apple juice
1	tablespoon lemon juice

Process celery and almonds using #2 cone, apple using #3 cone.
Preheat skillet on medium heat; add almonds, stir until golden brown. Remove from skillet; set aside.
Place rice in skillet, stir constantly until hot; reduce heat to low; slowly add apple juice and lemon juice. Cover; cook over medium heat until Vapo-Valve clicks, reduce heat to low and cook 40 minutes. Add celery, cover and cook 10 minutes more or until liquid is absorbed and rice is tender. Add apple and almonds. Serve immediately.

1 serving contains:

Cal	Prot	Fat	Carb	Fiber	Chol	Sodium
209	3.8 g	7.7 g	33.6 g	3.3 g	0 mg	24.9 mg

Brown Rice Pilaf

Utensils: 2-quart saucepan, Saladmaster Machine
Yield: 4 servings

1	small carrot
8	small fresh mushrooms
1/2	teaspoon instant chicken bouillon
1	cup water
3/4	cup quick-cooking brown rice
1/4	teaspoon dried marjoram
1/8	teaspoon freshly ground black pepper
1/4	cup thinly sliced green onion
2	tablespoon snipped fresh parsley

Process carrot using #1 cone, mushrooms use #2 cone.
In saucepan stir together bouillon and water, bring to boil over medium heat. Stir in mushrooms, brown rice, carrot, marjoram and

Brown Rice Pilaf, Cont.

pepper. Cover; cook over medium heat until Vapo-Valve clicks, reduce heat to low and simmer 40-45 minutes or until all liquid is absorbed and rice is tender. Remove from heat; let stand 5 minutes. Add green onion and parsley; toss lightly with fork. Serve immediately.

1 serving contains:

Cal	Prot	Fat	Carb	Fiber	Chol	Sodium
156	3.9 g	1.2 g	32.9 g	2.3 g	0.0003 mg	17.9 mg

Stovetop Baked Potatoes

A unique, simple way that captures potatoes true taste and nutrition.

Utensil: Large skillet;
Yield: 8 servings

4   medium potatoes

Cut potatoes in half, make a "cross" into meat side of each potato half; wipe dry with paper towel. Place meat side down in skillet. Cover; cook over medium heat until Vapo-Valve clicks, reduce heat to low and cook 30 minutes.

1 serving contains:

Cal	Prot	Fat	Carb	Fiber	Chol	Sodium
38	1.1 g	0.05 g	8.6 g	0.3 g	0 mg	1.5 mg

Low-cal toppings: Fluff potatoes using a fork. Top as desired.

- **fat-free or reduced-fat sour cream**
- **grated fat-free Cheddar, mozzarella or Monterrey jack cheese with peppers**
- **fat-free cottage cheese**
- **sliced green onions**
- **salsa or chow chow**
- **chopped green chilies**
- **low-fat chili**
- **spaghetti sauce and grated Parmesan cheese**

- mushrooms, fresh or canned, heated in liquid butter substitute
- chutney
- chopped broccoli in low-fat cheese sauce

Fresh Steamed Asparagus with Almonds

Asparagus was once only grown in Europe and Asia, where its young shoots were prized as a vegetable. We offer it here in one of its simplest yet most delicious forms.

Utensils: 3-quart saucepan, Steamer Inset, small gourmet skillet
Yield: 4 servings

2	pounds fresh asparagus
4	cups water
1	(2-ounce) package slivered almonds
1	teaspoon margarine

Wash fresh asparagus and snap off tough stem ends.

Pour water in saucepan; bring to boil over medium heat. Place fresh asparagus in steamer inset; place over boiling water. Cover; steam 4-5 minutes or until barely tender.

In small skillet, melt margarine over low heat. Add almonds; saute. Top fresh asparagus with sauteed almonds before serving.

1 serving contains:

Cal	Prot	Fat	Carb	Fiber	Chol	Sodium
143	9.8 g	8.9 g	11.3 g	4.8 g	0 mg	18.2 mg

Easy veggies

Follow the method in this recipe substituting a package of carrot, cabbage or broccoli slaw. These convenience products are usually found in the produce section. Omit cinnamon when substituting shredded broccoli. Nutmeg is a surprising flavor complement for the green cruciferous vegetable, however.

Orange Spiced Rice

Utensils: 3-quart saucepan, Saladmaster Machine
Yield: 8 servings

1	**small onion**
2	**celery stalks**
2	**medium oranges**
2	**teaspoons olive oil**
2	**cups brown rice**
3	**cups water**
2	**cups chicken broth**
2/3	**cup golden raisins**

Process onion and celery using #1 cone, grate peel of 1 orange by holding fruit against #1 cone, peel second orange; cut both oranges into small segments.

Pour oil in saucepan, set on medium-low heat. Add onion and celery, saute 3 minutes. Add rice; saute 2 minutes, stirring frequently. Add water, broth, raisins and 1 teaspoon grated orange peel. Cover; bring to boil. When Vapo-Valve clicks, reduce heat to low and simmer 40-45 minutes, or until liquid is absorbed and rice is tender. Add orange segments, serve immediately.

1 serving contains:

Cal	Prot	Fat	Carb	Fiber	Chol	Sodium
260	6.1 g	3 g	53.6 g	3.8 g	0.3 mg	208 mg

Spell peel z-e-s-t

When a recipe calls for orange or lemon zest, it means grated peel. When grating citrus peel, use just the outer, colored portions. The white part, called pith, is bitter. Using grated peel gives a true orange, lemon or even lime flavor without the acid of the juice. Grated peel is particularly useful in vegetable recipes, with meat, fish or baked goods.

Corn on the Cob

Frozen
Utensil: Large skillet
Yield: 6 servings

6 ears sweet corn

Saturate paper towel with water; place in bottom of skillet. Place corn on paper towel. Cover; cook over medium heat until Vapo-Valve clicks, reduce heat to low and cook 12-15 minutes.

Fresh
Utensils: Large skillet, 11-inch utility rack, high dome cover
Yield: 4 servings

4 ears sweet corn
4 cups water

Shuck sweet corn; cut in half and wash. Pour water into skillet; insert utility rack. Bring water to boil on medium heat, place corn on rack. Cover with high dome cover; steam for 15-20 minutes.

To use the corn shucks, rinse enough shucks to cover bottom of skillet, (leave plenty of moisture on shucks), place corn on shucks. Cover; cook over medium heat until Vapo-Valve clicks, reduce heat to low and cook 10-15 minutes.

1 serving contains:

Cal	Prot	Fat	Carb	Fiber	Chol	Sodium
83	2.6 g	1 g	19.4 g	3.2 g	0 mg	13 mg

Butternut Squash

Utensils: Small skillet, Saladmaster Machine
Yield: 4 servings

1 large butternut squash
1/2 tablespoon margarine
1/4 teaspoon nutmeg
1/4 teaspoon cinnamon

Butternut Squash, Cont.

Quarter squash lengthwise, remove seeds.
Process squash using #1 cone (keeping rind away from cone to peel). Place in skillet. Cover; cook over medium-low heat until Vapo-Valve clicks, reduce heat to low and cook for about 15 minutes. Add margarine, nutmeg and cinnamon, stir.

1 serving contains:

Cal	Prot	Fat	Carb	Fiber	Chol	Sodium
106	2.1 g	1.7 g	24 g	6.4 g	0 mg	27 mg

Stuffed Winter Squash

Utensils: 3-quart saucepan, Steamer Inset, Saladmaster Machine
Yield: 4 servings

1	ounce fresh Parmesan cheese
1/2	small onion
1/2	small zucchini
1/2	small carrot
1	small apple
1/2	teaspoon dried tarragon
1/8	teaspoon freshly ground black pepper
1	acorn or butternut squash, halved and seeded
4	cups water

Process cheese using #1 cone, onion using #2 cone, zucchini, carrot and apple using #3 cone.

In a medium bowl mix cheese, onion, zucchini, carrot, apple, tarragon and pepper. Stuff squash halves with vegetable mixture; place in Steamer Inset. Pour water in saucepan; cover, bring to boil over medium heat. Place steamer over boiling water. Cover; cook over medium heat until Vapo-Valve clicks, reduce heat to low and steam 20 minutes.

1 serving contains:

Cal	Prot	Fat	Carb	Fiber	Chol	Sodium
174	5.8 g	2.6 g	36.2 g	8.6 g	5.5 mg	144 mg

Toppings: For even more flavor consider a dollop of:
- natural applesauce
- fat-free sour cream
- yogurt cream

Autumn Acorn Squash Rings

Utensil: Large skillet
Yield: 4 servings

1	**small-to-medium acorn squash**
2	**teaspoons margarine**
1	**tablespoon dark brown sugar**
1	**tablespoon *apple juice or cider**
	dash of freshly grated nutmeg

Trim stem end and tip of squash, remove seeds. Cut into 4 slices.

Melt margarine in skillet over medium heat, stir in brown sugar and apple juice. Arrange squash rings in one layer in bottom of pan. Sprinkle lightly with nutmeg.

Cover; cook over medium heat. When Vapo-Valve clicks, reduce heat to low and cook 13-15 minutes or until squash is tender. Remove cover and turn squash to glaze remaining sides. If necessary, simmer off any excess moisture over medium heat, then serve.

1 serving contains:

Cal	Prot	Fat	Carb	Fiber	Chol	Sodium
95.6	1.3	2.1 g	20.4 g	3.2 g	0 mg	32.1 mg

The real thing

Try substituting a tablespoon of pure maple syrup for the brown sugar in this recipe. A dash of maple syrup (it has to be the real thing, not maple-flavored syrup) gives squash and almost any other vegetable a fresher, just-picked taste. Use instead of sugar for a more natural flavor boost. A touch of maple syrup also does wonders for smoothing the flavor of salsa or any dish with peppers that may be too hot.

French-Cut Beans Almondine

Utensils: Small skillet, 2-quart saucepan
Yield: 4 servings

1	**pound green beans**
1/4	**cup sliced almonds**
1	**teaspoon margarine**
2	**tablespoons fresh parsley, minced**

Prepare green beans by cutting 2-inch pieces on very sharp diagonal. Place almonds in small skillet, stir over low heat until lightly browned; set aside and let pan cool completely.

Rinse and drain green beans in saucepan. Cover; cook over medium heat until Vapo-Valve clicks, reduce heat to low and cook about 8-10 minutes, just until beans are firm-tender. Toss with margarine, almonds and parsley. Serve hot.

1 serving contains:

Cal	Prot	Fat	Carb	Fiber	Chol	Sodium
98.7	3.9 g	5.7 g	10.8 g	4 g	0 mg	18.1 mg

Chunky Carrots and Parsnips

Utensil: 1-quart saucepan
Yield: 4 servings

3	**small carrots**
2	**small parsnips**
1	**green onion, white portion only, thinly sliced**
1	**tablespoon margarine (optional)**
2	**tablespoons fresh parsley, minced**
1	**tablespoon fresh basil, minced (optional)**
1	**teaspoon lemon juice**

Cut carrots and parsnips in half lengthwise, then cut into 1-inch pieces. (Discard cores of parsnips if they are "woody.") Place carrots and parsnips in saucepan; rinse and drain, add green onion. Cover; cook over medium heat until Vapo-Valve clicks, reduce heat to low and cook 10-15 minutes, or until vegetables are barely tender.

Remove from heat. Add margarine, herbs, and lemon juice, toss gently. Serve hot.

1 serving contains:

Cal	Prot	Fat	Carb	Fiber	Chol	Sodium
29.6	0.7 g	0.1 g	7 g	2.1 g	0 mg	20.2 mg

Carrot Nests with Peas

Utensil: 2-quart saucepan
Yield: 4 servings

4	medium carrots
1/4	cup frozen peas
	dash of ground cinnamon
	dash of freshly grated nutmeg

Use vegetable peeler to cut very long, thin shreds of carrot, 1/4 - 1/2 inch wide. Place shredded carrots in saucepan, rinse, and drain. Push to one side.

Place peas in pan next to shredded carrots. Cover and cook over medium heat until Vapo-Valve clicks, turn heat to low, and cook 1-2 minutes, just until vegetables are firm-tender.

To serve, toss carrots with a dash of cinnamon and nutmeg. Arrange carrots into 4 "nests." Place 1 tablespoon peas in each nest. Serve hot.

1 serving contains:

Cal	Prot	Fat	Carb	Fiber	Chol	Sodium
74.1	2.1 g	0.3 g	16.9 g	5.6 g	0 mg	106 mg

Broccoli with Lemon-Dill Sauce

Utensils: 2-quart saucepan, Saladmaster Machine;
Yield: 4 servings

1	lemon
2	stalks broccoli
1/3	cup chicken broth
1	teaspoon cornstarch
2	tablespoons fresh dillweed, minced

Broccoli with Lemon-Dill Sauce, Cont.

Cut stems off broccoli and separate florets.

Grate peel of lemon by holding against #1 cone; squeeze juice from lemon. Process broccoli stalks using #2 cone.

Place florets and processed stalks in saucepan, rinse, and drain. Cover; cook over medium heat until Vapo-Valve clicks, reduce heat to low, and cook 5-7 minutes, until broccoli is crisp-tender. Remove to serving dish and keep warm.

Using the same pan combine broth, 2 tablespoons lemon juice, and cornstarch; bring to a boil over medium heat, stirring frequently. Reduce heat to low, stirring until sauce is thickened. Remove from heat and stir in 1/4 teaspoon lemon rind and dillweed. Pour sauce over broccoli and serve.

● ●

1 serving contains:

Cal	Prot	Fat	Carb	Fiber	Chol	Sodium
56.4	5.6 g	0.7 g	10.8 g	5.9 g	0.1 mg	110 mg

● ●

Parslied Carrots and Broccoli: Use 1-2 stalks broccoli, depending on size, and 2 carrots, cut in julienne strips using #2 cone. Prepare as in basic recipe above, substituting minced parsley for dill in sauce.

German Red Cabbage with Apples

This tart, colorful dish is a favorite at German restaurants and festivals. It's a quick dish to prepare and goes well with a variety of meats, especially pork chops.

Utensils: 3 or 4-quart saucepan, Saladmaster Machine;
Yield: 6 servings

1	**2 - 2 1/2-pound red cabbage**
2	**medium, tart green apples, cored**
1 1/2	**small onions**
2	**whole cloves**
1/3	**cup red wine vinegar**
1 1/2	**tablespoons brown sugar**
1/4	**teaspoon salt**
1	**bay leaf**
3	**tablespoons *dry red wine or apple cider**
3	**tablespoons *red currant or plum jelly**

Quarter cabbage lengthwise, process using #5 cone, apples useing #4 cone, process $1/2$ of an onion using #2 cone. Stick cloves in whole onion.
Place cabbage in saucepan, sprinkle with vinegar, brown sugar, and salt, then toss to coat cabbage. Let stand 5 minutes. Add apples, chopped onions, whole onion stuck with cloves, bay leaf, and wine or cider. Stir thoroughly. Cover; cook over medium heat until Vapo-Valve clicks, reduce heat to low and cook 20 minutes or until tender.
Remove whole onion with cloves and bay leaf. Stir in currant jelly, heat 2-3 minutes until jelly is thoroughly mixed in. Serve hot.

1 serving contains:

Cal	Prot	Fat	Carb	Fiber	Chol	Sodium
105	2.9 g	0.7 g	24.6 g	5.9 g	0 mg	114 mg

Two-Minute Cherry Tomatoes

For a quick, colorful side dish, these tiny tomatoes have no competition.

Utensil: Small skillet;
Yield: 4 servings

2	cups cherry tomatoes
2	tablespoons *fresh parsley or fresh basil, minced

Place tomatoes in small skillet, cover and cook over medium heat until Vapo-Valve clicks. Turn heat to low, and cook 2 minutes, just until tomatoes are heated through. Sprinkle with parsley or basil and serve hot.

1 serving contains:

Cal	Prot	Fat	Carb	Fiber	Chol	Sodium
19.6	0.8 g	0.3 g	4.3 g	1.4 g	0 mg	8.8 mg

Honey-Minted Cherry Tomatoes: Cook as in basic recipe above. When done, stir in 1 teaspoon honey and 1 tablespoon minced fresh mint or $1/2$ tablespoon crumbled dried mint leaves over medium heat until evenly distributed. Serve hot.

Wild Rice Pilaf

Utensils: 1-quart saucepan, Saladmaster Machine;
Yield: 4-6 servings

1	**small carrot**
1	**medium onion**
1	**celery stalk**
1	**tablespoon margarine**
3/4	**cup brown rice**
1/4	**cup wild rice**
1 1/2	**cups chicken broth**
1	**tablespoon lemon juice**
3	**tablespoons fresh parsley, minced**

Process carrot using #1 cone, onion and celery using #2 cone.
Melt margarine in saucepan over medium heat. Add carrot, onion, and celery, stir one minute. Add brown and wild rice, stir. Add broth and lemon juice. Cover; cook over medium heat until Vapo-Valve clicks, reduce heat to low and cook 40-45 minutes or until liquid is absorbed and rice is tender. Remove from heat, stir in parsley, place in warmed serving bowl.

1 serving contains:

Cal	Prot	Fat	Carb	Fiber	Chol	Sodium
143	4.1 g	3.1 g	25 g	2.3 g	0.3 mg	238 mg

Tomato hors d'ouevres

Use small, firm tomatoes. Cut off tops and scoop out seeds using a melon baller. Fill with thawed spinach souffle (sold in the frozen food counter). Proceed according to recipe, making sure the souffle is heated through.

Spaghetti Squash Carnivale

Vegetarian Main Dishes

More and more health-conscious cooks prepare meatless meals a couple of times per week. Vegetarian dishes are tasteful, economical and an easy way to increase vitamin and fiber consumption.

Of course, summer is a great time to prepare vegetable meals. That's when farmers' markets are loaded with vine-ripe tomatoes, squash, onions, peas and beans. Substitute liberally in these recipes, using what is in season and your favorite vegetables.

Vegetarian dishes can be part of a complete and balanced diet because of the "complementary proteins" often found in traditional meatless dishes. For centuries, cultures have flourished with little or no meat in their diets. But vegetable dishes can provide "complete" protein, almost the nutritional equal to that found in meat and eggs. Persons on a totally vegetarian diet usually do some vitamin supplementation, but an occasional meatless meal provides more than adequate nutrients and protein.

What's required is the combination of complementary proteins found in vegetables, such as beans, and in grains, such as rice or corn. Not surprisingly, those combinations are natural and tasty.

Vegetarian main dishes are a good way to try to reach those goals. One of the other principles of meatless eating involves what is called "protein combining." The building blocks of protein (called amino acids) in bean dishes, for example, combine with those in complementary starches. Some other examples are lentils with rice, Chinese stir-fry with tofu (bean curd) or a peanut butter sandwich.

Since beans can be such an important part of meatless meals, knowing how to cook dried beans and legumes can be very helpful. When time doesn't allow for soaking and cooking, consider using canned beans. Their texture is very similar to cooked beans and the time saved is significant.

How to cook dried beans and legumes

Rinse beans well and place in enough water to cover generously. Remember that beans will double in bulk after several hours of soaking.

- Look for shriveled or damaged beans; remove any that float.
- Soak beans for 6 to 8 hours or overnight.
- Drain beans and refill pan with enough water to cover. Place pan over medium heat and cover. When Vapo-Valve clicks, reduce heat to low and cook according to the table below.

Bean Chart

Type of Dried	Bean Soaking Time	Cooking Time (in hrs.)
Black beans	Overnight or quick soak	1 1/2
Chick-peas	Overnight or quick soak	3
Kidney beans	Overnight or quick soak	1 1/2
Lentils	None	45 minutes
Lima beans	Overnight or quick soak	1 1/2
Navy beans	None	1 1/2
Soybeans	Overnight or quick soak	3 or more
Split peas	None	1 hour

Cuban Black Beans and Rice

Utensil: 7-quart Dutch oven
Yield: 8 servings

1 1/2	cups black beans
3	quarts water
2	hot green or red chili peppers, halved and seeded
2	cloves garlic
1	small red or green pepper, quartered
5	medium tomatoes, divided
1	large onion, quartered
2	bay leaves
2	tablespoons reduced-sodium soy sauce
2	tablespoons olive oil
2	tablespoons vinegar
8	cups cooked rice
2	green onions, thinly sliced on diagonal
2	tablespoons fresh parsley, minced

Place beans and 2 quarts of water in Dutch oven. Cover; soak overnight. Drain.

Chop one tomato; cut remaining 4 into wedges.

Place $1/2$ cup water in blender and add hot peppers, garlic, red pepper, chopped tomato, and onion. Blend on medium speed until smooth.

Add remaining water, bay leaves, and blended mixture to beans. Cover; cook over medium heat until Vapo-Valve clicks, reduce heat to low and cook 1 $1/2$ hours or until beans are tender. Remove bay leaves, discard; stir in soy sauce, oil, and vinegar.

To serve: Spread rice on serving platter. Spoon beans over rice. Arrange quartered tomatoes around outside of platter and top with green onions and parsley.

1 serving contains:

Cal	Prot	Fat	Carb	Fiber	Chol	Sodium
372	9.9 g	4.5 g	72.8 g	5.5 g	0 mg	133 mg

Vegetarian Wok

Utensils: Wok, Saladmaster Machine
Yield: 4 servings

1	medium yellow squash
2	medium carrots
1	small green pepper
1	small onion
1	teaspoon olive oil
1	whole garlic clove
1	medium zucchini, cut into long strips
1	cup broccoli florets
1	teaspoon gingerroot, minced
1	(8-ounce) can sliced water chestnuts
1/4	cup reduced-sodium soy sauce
1	(8-ounce) can pineapple chunks, packed in its own juice, drained
1	(6-ounce) can mandarin oranges, drained

Process squash, carrots, green pepper and onion using #4 cone.

Heat oil in wok over medium-high heat. Add garlic clove; sear and remove. Do not brown. Add squash, carrots, green pepper, onion, zucchini and broccoli in wok; stir together 5 minutes. Add gingerroot, water

Vegetarian Wok, Cont.

chestnuts, soy sauce and fruit. Cover; cook 2 minutes. Remove from heat; let set 5 minutes. Serve over brown rice.

1 serving contains:

Cal	Prot	Fat	Carb	Fiber	Chol	Sodium
164	4.8 g	1.7 g	36.3 g	6.4 g	0 mg	508 mg

Zucchini Lasagna

All the benefits of Saladmaster are rolled into this one fast, easy, and nutritious recipe.

Utensils: Large skillet or Electric skillet, Saladmaster Machine
Yield: 6 servings

8	ounces reduced-fat or *fat-free mozzarella cheese
1	small onion
1	medium zucchini
1	cup loosely packed, fresh spinach
2	tablespoons olive oil
2	green onions, thinly sliced
1	egg or 2 egg whites, or *$1/2$ cup egg substitute
16	ounces fat-free cottage cheese
4	cups tomato sauce
6-8	lasagna noodles, broken in half, uncooked
2	tablespoons fresh parsley, minced, garnish

Process cheese using #2 cone, onion and zucchini using #4 cone, spinach using #5 cone.

Heat oil in skillet over medium heat, add onion, stirring until tender. Add green onions and spinach, stir until wilted. Remove from skillet, set aside.

Let skillet cool

In a medium bowl lightly beat egg; add cottage cheese, stir, set aside.

In cold skillet layer ingredients in the following order:
1 cup tomato sauce
Arrange single layer of zucchini, slightly overlapped
$1/2$ uncooked noodles

1 cup tomato sauce
cottage cheese-egg mixture
remaining noodles
onion and spinach mixture
remaining tomato sauce
mozzarella cheese

Cover; cook 25-30 minutes at 225 degrees. Turn control off and let stand 10 minutes or until set.

1 serving contains:

Cal	Prot	Fat	Carb	Fiber	Chol	Sodium
343	31.2 g	7.6 g	40.3 g	4.7 g	10.4 mg	1590 mg

Spaghetti Squash Carnivale

Utensils: 3-quart saucepan, Steamer Inset, Large skillet, Saladmaster Machine
Yield: 6 servings

1	ounce Parmesan cheese
1	medium onion
2	small zucchini
1	cup loosely packed fresh spinach
4	cups water
1	2-pound spaghetti squash
2	tablespoons olive oil
1	green pepper, cut in 2-inch strips
1	red pepper, cut in 2-inch strips
1/4	cup fresh basil leaves, chopped
2	tablespoons fresh parsley, minced
1	cup cooked chick-peas
1	cup tomato sauce
	dash of freshly ground black pepper

Process cheese using #1 cone, onion and zucchini using #4 cone, spinach using #5 cone.

Pour water in saucepan, bring to boil over medium heat. Place whole squash in steamer and insert into saucepan. Cover; steam for 30 minutes or until tender.

Spaghetti Squash Carnivale, Cont.

While squash is cooking: Heat skillet over medium heat until drops of water dance when sprinkled in pan, add oil. When oil is hot, add onion, green and red peppers; cook quickly until crisp-tender, about 3-4 minutes. Add zucchini, spinach, basil, and parsley, stir until spinach is wilted. Add chick-peas, tomato sauce, and pepper; stir. Cover; cook until Vapo-Valve clicks, reduce heat to low and cook 5 minutes. Remove from heat.

When squash is tender, using a serrated knife and holding squash with potholder, cut in half lengthwise. Scoop out seeds. With a fork, scrape spaghetti-like strands from squash. Arrange squash strands in a large shallow serving dish. Spoon hot sauce over squash, sprinkle with Parmesan cheese.

1 serving contains:

Cal	Prot	Fat	Carb	Fiber	Chol	Sodium
232	9 g	7.5 g	36 g	10.9 g	3.7 mg	391 mg

Savory Lentil Tacos

Utensils: 3-quart saucepan, Saladmaster Machine
Yield: 4 servings

2	ounces reduced-fat or *fat-free sharp Cheddar cheese
1	small onion
1/4	head lettuce
1/2	cup dried lentils
2	cloves garlic, minced
1 3/4	cups water
1 1/2	teaspoons chili powder
1/4	teaspoon cumin
1/4	cup tomato paste
1	teaspoon molasses
8	taco shells
1/2	cup thinly sliced green onions
1	cup Tomato Salsa (This recipe can be found on page 1-20)

Process cheese using #1 cone, onion using #2 cone, lettuce using #5 cone; cover lettuce and refrigerate until ready to use.

Place lentils, onion, garlic, and water in large saucepan. Cover; cook over medium heat until Vapo-Valve clicks, reduce heat to low and cook 25 minutes.

Stir in chili powder, cumin, tomato paste, and molasses.

Cover; increase heat to medium, cook until Vapo-Valve clicks, reduce heat to low and cook 20 minutes more; or until lentils are tender, but not mushy.

Spoon 3-4 tablespoons of the lentil mixture into each taco shell. Top with cheese, lettuce, green onions, and salsa.

1 serving contains:

Cal	Prot	Fat	Carb	Fiber	Chol	Sodium
311	17 g	6.7 g	53.2 g	9.9 g	2.5 mg	388 mg

California Pasta

Utensils: Dutch oven, Large skillet, Saladmaster Machine
Yield: 4 servings

4	ounces reduced-fat or *fat-free sharp Cheddar cheese
1/2	pound fresh whole wheat pasta
1	small onion, quartered
1	small carrot, quartered
1/2	red pepper
1/2	cup water
2	cups low-sodium tomato sauce
1	small head cauliflower, separated into florets
1/4	teaspoon dried marjoram
	dash of cayenne pepper

Process cheese using #1 cone.

Using Dutch oven prepare pasta according to package directions; drain, set aside.

Place onion, carrot, and red pepper in food processor or blender with water, process smooth, pour into skillet. Cover; cook over medium heat until Vapo-Valve clicks, reduce heat to low and cook 10 minutes.

Increase heat to medium, add tomato sauce, cauliflower, marjoram, and cayenne. Cover; cook until Vapo-Valve clicks, reduce heat to low, and cook 6-8 minutes or until cauliflower is tender.

Arrange pasta in a large pasta bowl, spoon vegetables over pasta, and sprinkle with cheese.

1 serving contains:

Cal	Prot	Fat	Carb	Fiber	Chol	Sodium
180	15.4 g	1.7 g	31.8 g	6.4 g	5.1 mg	248 mg

Garden Tortillas

Utensils: Small skillet, 2-quart saucepan, Saladmaster Machine
Yield: 4 servings

2	**ounces reduced-fat or *fat-free sharp Cheddar cheese**
1	**small zucchini**
1/2	**small green pepper**
6	**fresh mushrooms**
1	**cup loosely packed, fresh spinach**
1/2	**cup broccoli florets, chopped**
1/4	**cup green onions, sliced**
1/2	**cup tomatoes**
4	**flour tortillas, chopped**
3/4	**cup Tomato Salsa** (This recipe can be found on page 1-20)

Process cheese using #1 cone, zucchini and green pepper using #2 cone, mushrooms and spinach using #5 cone.

Place all vegetables in saucepan; rinse and drain. Cover; cook over medium heat until Vapo-Valve clicks, reduce heat to low and cook 2-3 minutes until vegetables are tender-crisp.

Heat small skillet on medium heat until drops of water dance when sprinkled in pan. Place one flour tortilla at a time in pan just long enough to heat on each side. Tortillas should not become crisp. Wrap in clean dish towel to keep warm.

To assemble tortillas, sprinkle each with 1 tablespoon cheese. Arrange one-fourth of the vegetable mixture down the center of each tortilla. Fold two sides of the tortilla over filling and place seam-side down on platter. Spoon salsa over tortillas and sprinkle with remaining cheese before serving.

1 serving contains:

Cal	Prot	Fat	Carb	Fiber	Chol	Sodium
194	10.7 g	3.5 g	34.5 g	5.3 g	2.5 mg	268 mg

Middle Eastern Burgers

Utensil: Large skillet
Yield: 4 servings

2	**tablespoons sesame seeds**
2	**tablespoons parsley**
1	**tablespoon olive oil**

1	tablespoon lemon juice
1	tablespoon reduced-sodium soy sauce
1	teaspoon cumin
1	teaspoon ground coriander
1/2	teaspoon chili powder
1	egg, or 2 egg whites or 1/4 cup egg substitute
1	cup cooked chick-peas
2/3	cup wheat germ or oat bran
	vegetable spray

Place sesame seeds in blender and blend until partially ground. Add parsley, oil, lemon juice, soy sauce, cumin, coriander, chili powder, and egg. Blend on low speed until smooth. Add chick-peas and continue blending on low speed.

When smooth, transfer mixture to medium bowl and stir in wheat germ or oat bran. Form mixture into four patties. Preheat skillet over medium-low heat; when hot, spray with vegetable spray. Place patties in skillet, cook until brown on both sides and burger is done, about 8-10 minutes.

• •

1 serving contains:

Cal	Prot	Fat	Carb	Fiber	Chol	Sodium
176	9.3 g	9.6 g	24.3 g	6.2 g	0.3 mg	159 mg

• •

Pita Pizza

This recipe places first with teenagers, who often serve it at casual parties. It's quick, tasty, and can be easily adapted to include their favorite ingredients.

Utensils: Small skillet, Saladmaster Machine;
Yield: 1 serving

1	ounce reduced-fat or *fat-free mozzarella cheese
1	pita pocket bread
1	tablespoon tomato paste
1/8	teaspoon dried basil
1/8	teaspoon dried oregano

Process cheese using #1 cone.

Spread pita bread to the edges with tomato paste. Crumble basil

Pita Pizza, Cont.

and oregano over tomato paste, then sprinkle with shredded cheese.
Place the pita pizza in small skillet. Set over medium-low heat
and cover. Bake 4-5 minutes, until cheese is melted and pita is
heated through.

• •

1 serving contains:

Cal	Prot	Fat	Carb	Fiber	Chol	Sodium
220	16 g	1.1 g	37.3 g	1.7 g	5.1 mg	671 mg

• •

Chili Non Carne

Utensils: 7-quart Dutch oven, Saladmaster Machine;
Yield: 10 servings

1	**pound dried kidney beans**
3	**quarts water**
2	**medium carrots**
2	**celery stalks**
2	**small onions**
3 1/2-4	**cups tomato sauce**
1	**large tomato, chopped**
1	**hot pepper, seeded and minced**
1	**medium red or green pepper, cubed**
1/4	**cup minced fresh parsley**
5	**cloves garlic, minced**
1/2	**teaspoon dried marjoram**
1	**teaspoon dried oregano**
1/4	**teaspoon cayenne pepper (or to taste)**
2	**bay leaves**

Place beans and 2 quarts of water in Dutch oven. Cover; soak overnight.
Drain.
Process carrots using #2 cone, celery and onion using #4 cone.
Return beans to Dutch oven; add remaining water. Cover; cook over
medium heat until Vapo-Valve clicks, reduce heat to low and cook 1
hour. Remove cover, add remaining ingredients, stir. Cover; increase
heat to medium and cook until Vapo-Valve clicks, reduce heat to low
and cook 1 hour, or until beans are tender. Remove bay leaves, discard.
Serve over rice for a protein-rich meal.

● ●
1 serving contains:

Cal	Prot	Fat	Carb	Fiber	Chol	Sodium
250	13.7 g	1 g	50.3 g	14.6 g	0 mg	622 mg

● ●

Beans are an excellent canned product. When time doesn't allow for starting with dried beans, substituting canned beans can be a real help. It is often a good idea to drain and rinse the beans since the packing liquid can sometimes be cloudy or add more liquid than you want in the dish. Consider black beans, pintos, kidney beans, black-eyed peas, navy beans and cannelloni beans.

How to cook rice

Place 1 cup rice and 2 cups water (or other liquid) in saucepan. Cover and place over medium-high heat. When Vapo-Valve clicks rapidly, turn heat to low and cook 15 minutes or until liquid is absorbed and rice is tender. (Brown and wild rice take longer than white rice. Some quick-cooking brands don't require cooking, just reconstituting with hot water.) If using salt, add after water has come to a boil and stir until it dissolves. This prevents damaging the surface of the pan.

Pasta San Marco

Utensils: 7-quart Dutch oven, Saladmaster Machine
Yield: 4 servings

2	ounces Parmesan cheese
1/2	cup walnuts
1/2	pound spaghetti, spirals, or shells
1 1/2	tablespoons olive oil
3	cloves garlic, minced
1	cup tomatoes, seeded and chopped
1/2	cup black olives, chopped
1/2	cup red pimiento, chopped
1/4	cup fresh parsley, chopped
3	tablespoons fresh basil or 1 teaspoon *dried basil, minced
1/4	teaspoon salt
	dash of freshly ground black pepper

Process cheese using #1 cone, walnuts using #3 cone.

Using the Dutch oven prepare pasta according to directions; drain. Set aside.

Place oil in hot Dutch oven, add garlic, stir with wooden spoon over low heat until slightly tender. Do not brown. Add walnuts, tomatoes, olives, pimiento, parsley, basil, salt and pepper to pan; stir. Cook only until hot. Arrange pasta in a large pasta bowl and spoon sauce over top, sprinkle with cheese.

● ●

1 serving contains:

Cal	Prot	Fat	Carb	Fiber	Chol	Sodium
469	18.2 g	22.3 g	51.3 g	6.1 g	11 mg	658 mg

● ●

Spanish-Style Vegetable Casserole

Utensil: 3-quart saucepan, Saladmaster Machine
Yield: 4 servings

1	medium onion
1	red or green pepper
1	small potato peeled
1	tablespoon olive oil
1	clove garlic, minced
1	medium tomato, chopped
$1/2$	teaspoon paprika
$1/4$	teaspoon cayenne pepper
1	cup long-grain rice
2	cups low-fat, low-sodium chicken broth
1	medium zucchini quartered lengthwise and cut into 3-inch pieces
2	medium carrots, halved lengthwise, and cut into 3-inch pieces
2	cups fresh or frozen green peas

Process onion, red pepper and potato using #2 cone.

Heat oil in saucepan over medium heat for 1 minute. Add onion and garlic, cook until tender. Add red pepper and tomato, cook 3 minutes. Add potato, paprika, and cayenne pepper, cook 2 minutes longer. Stir in rice and chicken broth. Cover; cook until Vapo-Valve clicks, reduce heat to low and cook for 15 minutes or until most of the liquid is absorbed. Stir in the zucchini, carrots, and peas, cover, cook for 10 minutes. Serve immediately.

● ●

1 serving contains:

Cal	Prot	Fat	Carb	Fiber	Chol	Sodium
332	10.9 g	4.4 g	62.5 g	7.2 g	0.4 mg	51.9 mg

● ●

Eggs Florentine

Utensil: Small skillet, Saladmaster Machine
Yield: 1 serving

1	cup loosely packed, fresh spinach
1/2	teaspoon *margarine or vegetable spray
2	eggs or 1/2 cup *egg substitute
1	additional egg white
1	tablespoon 2% or *skim milk
1	teaspoon minced fresh dillweed or *basil
1	tablespoon reduced-fat or *fat-free cottage cheese

Process spinach using #5 cone.

Melt margarine in skillet over medium heat, add spinach. Cover; cook until Vapo-Valve clicks, reduce heat to low and cook 1 minute, just until spinach is wilted.

Meanwhile: In a small bowl beat eggs, additional egg white and milk with fork. Increase heat to medium. Pour eggs over spinach, add dill; stir occasionally with wooden spoon until eggs are almost cooked through. Gently fold in cottage cheese and serve immediately.

● ●

1 serving contains:

Cal	Prot	Fat	Carb	Fiber	Chol	Sodium
256	21.3 g	15.5 g	8.2 g	2.1 g	2.9 g	426 mg

● ●

Golden Buttermilk Pancakes

Breakfasts and Breads

Breakfast has been called the most important meal of the day. All too often, it is the most neglected. Too many of us skip it altogether; others rely on over-processed convenience foods. Besides being short on nutrients, many such foods are expensive.

For nutrition and value, a homemade breakfast is often the best choice. And it doesn't have to be time-consuming.

Of course, breakfast can be a special time as well, even an occasion for entertaining. Don't overlook the potential for brunch to celebrate with family or friends.

The recipes in this chapter will serve you well every day. You'll also find delicious ideas for special occasion meals.

Nutrition and good taste are the main criteria for selection. We've eliminated unnecessary calories and fat without sacrificing flavor.

Remember when selecting breakfast foods that eggs can be part of a prudent diet. However, experts recommend limiting eggs to three or four per week, including eggs used in baking and other dishes.

You may choose to use cholesterol-free egg substitutes or remove yolks from whole eggs for most recipes. We give you instructions for doing that.

Regardless of whether a breakfast includes an egg dish, it is important to include whole grain breads or cereals and plenty of fruit in the menu. Limiting saturated fat, such as that found in bacon and sausage, is another important tool for good nutrition. It is helpful to use small amounts for flavoring. Canadian bacon is a good choice, for a lean breakfast meat.

Peasant Porridge

Utensil: 1-quart saucepan
Yield: 2 servings

1/2	cup bulgur
1	cup water
2	tablespoons raisins
1	teaspoon *brown sugar or unsulfured molasses
1/2	cup 2% or *skim milk (or as desired)

Place bulgur, water, and raisins in 1-quart saucepan. Cover; cook over medium heat until Vapo-Valve clicks, reduce heat to low, and cook 15 minutes. Remove cover and stir.
Add brown sugar or molasses and milk. Serve hot.
Also delicious with 1/2 cup fresh, sliced strawberries.

1 serving contains:

Cal	Prot	Fat	Carb	Fiber	Chol	Sodium
98.9	3.8 g	0.3 g	21.8 g	0.6 g	1 mg	35.9 mg

Basic Scrambled Eggs

Utensil: Small skillet
Yield: 2 servings

3	eggs or 3/4 cup *egg substitute
1	tablespoon 2% or *skim milk
	dash of salt
	dash of paprika
	*vegetable spray (or 1 teaspoon margarine, if desired)

Eggs should be at room temperature. In a medium bowl combine eggs, milk, salt and paprika. Beat with a whisk or fork until frothy.
Preheat skillet over medium heat, spray with vegetable spray. When hot add egg mixture, stirring occasionally with wooden spoon until eggs thicken into soft curds. Serve immediately.

1 serving contains:

Cal	Prot	Fat	Carb	Fiber	Chol	Sodium
147	10.4 g	10 g	3.3 g	0.03 g	1.6 mg	317 mg

Corn Cakes

Utensils: Large skillet, electric skillet, or 11 inch griddle
Yield: Approx. 12 cakes

1	**box corn muffin mix**
	vegetable spray

Prepare according to package instructions. Thin with additional liquid to desired consistency.

Preheat skillet over medium heat, spray with vegetable spray. When hot, spoon 1-2 tablespoons of batter into skillet for each corn cake. Cook until top begins to bubble and bottom is brown. Turn and continue to cook until both sides are brown. Serve cakes with honey or your choice of topping.

1 serving contains:

Cal	Prot	Fat	Carb	Fiber	Chol	Sodium
130	2.8 g	4.2 g	20 g	0 g	0 mg	192 mg

Apricot-Rice Breakfast Cereal

Utensil: 1-quart saucepan
Yield: 4 servings

1	**cup apple juice**
2	**cups cooked, leftover brown or *white rice**
2	**tablespoons chopped dried apricots**
1	**teaspoon maple syrup or *honey**
1	**cup 2% or *skim milk (or as desired)**

Stir apple juice, rice, and apricots together in 1-quart saucepan. Cover; cook over medium heat until Vapo-Valve clicks, reduce heat to low and cook 15 minutes. Stir.

Add maple syrup or honey and milk. Serve hot.

1 serving contains:

Cal	Prot	Fat	Carb	Fiber	Chol	Sodium
192	5 g	0.5 g	41.4 g	0.5 g	1 mg	35.5 mg

Oatmeal

Utensil: 1-quart saucepan
Yield: 2 servings

1 $^1/_2$	**cups water**
$^2/_3$	**cup old-fashioned rolled oats**
$^1/_2$	**cup 2% or *skim milk (or as desired)**
	sweetener, as desired

Place water and oats in 1-quart saucepan. Cover; cook over medium heat until Vapo-Valve clicks, reduce heat to low and cook 3-4 minutes.
Let stand an additional 2-3 minutes, if desired, for thicker porridge. Serve with milk and sweetener if desired. Serve hot.

• •

1 serving contains:

Cal	Prot	Fat	Carb	Fiber	Chol	Sodium
124	6.4 g	1.8 g	20.9 g	2.9 g	1 mg	32.6 mg

• •

Date and Walnut Oatmeal: Add 6 chopped, pitted dates, 1 tablespoon chopped walnuts, and 2 teaspoons maple syrup. Cook as above.

Making oatmeal special
Add along with oatmeal and water:
- **dried cranberries, cherries or blueberries**
- **all-bran**
- **wheat germ**
- **substitute apple juice for all or some of the water**
- **substitute skim milk for all of some of the water**
- **chopped fresh peaches**
- **chopped fresh apples**

Foolproof Omelet

Utensil: Small skillet
Yield: 2 servings

3	**eggs or $^3/_4$ cup *egg substitute**
1	**tablespoon 2% or *skim milk**
	dash of salt
	dash of paprika
	vegetable spray (or margarine, if desired)

Place eggs in medium bowl. Beat with electric mixer or whisk for 1 minute or until frothy, add milk, salt and paprika, beat just until combined. Preheat skillet on medium heat, spray with vegetable spray. When hot, add egg mixture, cover and cook over low heat, undisturbed 8-9 minutes. Remove lid, fold omelet in half, cut into two portions, and serve.

1 serving contains:

Cal	Prot	Fat	Carb	Fiber	Chol	Sodium
147	10.4 g	10 g	3.3 g	0.03	1.6 mg	317 mg

Cheese Omelet: Sprinkle ¹/₄ cup shredded reduced-fat or fat-free cheese over top of cooked omelet before folding and serving. *Herbed Omelet:* Beat 1 tablespoon minced fresh parsley and ¹/₂ teaspoon minced fresh basil (or ¹/₈ teaspoon dried) into eggs before cooking. *Mushroom Omelet:* Fold ¹/₃ cup cooked mushrooms into cooked omelet before serving. *Salsa Omelet:* Fold ¹/₃ cup Tomato Salsa into cooked omelet. *Sweet Lemon Omelet:* Omit milk and paprika, and beat 2 teaspoons honey, 1 teaspoon lemon juice, ¹/₂ teaspoon finely grated lemon rind, and ¹/₄ teaspoon vanilla extract into eggs before cooking.

Whole Wheat Cereal

Utensils: Large skillet, (or electric skillet,) 11 inch Rack, Pudding pan, High dome cover
Yield: 6 servings

2	cups whole grain wheat
3	cups water
	sugar or honey
	2% or skim milk

Place 3 cups water into skillet, place 11" rack in skillet. Put 2 cups wheat and 3 cups water into pudding pan and place on rack; cover with high dome cover. Cook on low heat. Let steam for 8 hours.

Add sugar or honey and milk, serve hot. (Try adding dried fruit the last 30 minutes)

1 serving contains:

Cal	Prot	Fat	Carb	Fiber	Chol	Sodium
221	8.8 g	1 g	47.7 g	8 g	0.3 mg	11.8 mg

French Toast

Utensil: Large skillet
Yield: 4 servings

1	whole egg or $^1/_4$ cup egg substitute
1	egg white
2	tablespoons 2% or skim milk
$^1/_2$	teaspoon vanilla extract
$^1/_4$	teaspoon cinnamon
4	large slices slightly stale, whole-grain bread
	vegetable spray (or margarine, if desired)

Place whole egg and egg white in a medium shallow bowl, beat with a whisk or fork until blended. Add milk, vanilla, and cinnamon; mix well.

Preheat skillet over medium heat, spray with vegetable spray. Dip slices of bread into egg mixture, coating both sides, and place in hot skillet. Cook until brown on both sides. Serve hot.

TOPPINGS: Try cinnamon applesauce, chopped fresh fruit and maple syrup, fruit sauces, or a light coating of fruit jam.

• •

1 serving contains:

Cal	Prot	Fat	Carb	Fiber	Chol	Sodium
118	6.3 g	3.2 g	17 g	2.6	0.4 mg	270 mg

• •

Potato Pancakes

Utensils: Large skillet or Electric skillet, Saladmaster Machine
Yield: 6 servings

3	medium potatoes
1	small onion
2	eggs or $^1/_2$ cup *egg substitute
$^1/_8$	teaspoon pepper
3	tablespoons 2% or *skim milk
$^1/_3$	cup all-purpose flour
$^1/_2$	teaspoon baking powder
$^1/_2$	teaspoon salt
	vegetable spray (or margarine, if desired)

Peel potatoes and onions, process using #1 cone.

In a large mixing bowl beat eggs; add pepper, potatoes, onions and milk; mix. Add flour, baking powder and salt to the potato mixture and mix well. (Add extra flour 1 tablespoon at a time to bind ingredients together.)

Preheat skillet over medium heat, spray with vegetable spray. When hot spoon 1-2 tablespoons of batter into skillet for each pancake. Cook until brown on each side; place lid on skillet, reduce heat to simmer and let cook to tenderize for about 2-3 minutes.

1 serving contains:

Cal	Prot	Fat	Carb	Fiber	Chol	Sodium
101	4.4 g	2.4 g	15.7 g	0.6 g	0.5 mg	251 mg

Garlic Bread

Enjoy the incomparably fresh taste of your own Skillet-baked Garlic Bread.

Utensil: Large skillet
Yield: 4 servings

1	clove garlic, minced
2	tablespoons olive oil
1/8	teaspoon salt
1/8	teaspoon freshly ground black pepper
2	tablespoons fresh parsley, finely minced
1/4	teaspoon dried marjoram
8	thick slices Italian bread

Combine garlic, oil, salt, pepper, parsley, and marjoram. Spread small amount on each bread slice. Heat large skillet 1-2 minutes over medium heat, then place bread slices, herbed side down, in one layer in skillet. Cook until very lightly toasted. (If garlic browns, it will become bitter.) Toast remaining bread slices. Serve hot.

1 serving contains:

Cal	Prot	Fat	Carb	Fiber	Chol	Sodium
228	5.5 g	7.3 g	34.2 g	1.14 g	0 mg	420 mg

Orange or Lemon Hotcakes

We would not dare print a cookbook without this beloved recipe. By popular request, it has been featured in our cookbooks for years!

Utensils: Large skillet, Electric skillet or 11 inch griddle
Yield: Approx. 12 cakes

1	box of orange or *lemon cake mix vegetable spray

Prepare according to package instructions. For thick hotcakes batter should be thick, add additional liquid for thinner hotcakes.

Preheat skillet over medium heat, spray skillet with vegetable spray. When hot spoon 1-2 tablespoons of batter into skillet for each hotcake. Cook until the top begins to bubble and underside is brown, turn and continue to cook until both sides are brown. Serve cakes with honey or your choice of topping.

1 serving contains:

Cal	Prot	Fat	Carb	Fiber	Chol	Sodium
260	3 g	11 g	36 g	0 g	55 mg	280 mg

Easy fruit sauces

Place 2 cups blueberries, strawberries, raspberries or blackberries and 1/3 cup light corn syrup or pure maple syrup in blender or food processor and process until smooth. Warm sauce in small saucepan over medium heat and cover with lid. When Vapo-Valve clicks, turn off heat. Let stand until ready to serve. Strain, if desired, to remove seeds. May serve hot or cold.

Golden Buttermilk Pancakes

Utensil: Large skillet or 11 inch griddle
Yield: 4 servings

2	cups unbleached flour
1	teaspoon baking powder
1/2	teaspoon baking soda
	dash of salt
1	egg or 1/4 cup *egg substitute, beaten
1 1/2-2	cups buttermilk
1	tablespoon vegetable oil (or less)
	vegetable spray

Combine flour, baking powder, baking soda, and salt in medium bowl. In small bowl, beat egg, add buttermilk and oil. Add liquid ingredients to flour mixture and stir just until mixed. For thick pancakes, begin with 1-1/2 cups buttermilk, add more buttermilk as desired.

Preheat skillet over medium heat, spray with vegetable spray. When hot pour 1/4 cup batter into pan with ladle to form each pancake. Cook pancakes until the top begins to bubble and underside is brown. Turn and continue to cook until both sides are brown. Repeat with remaining batter. Serve pancakes with choice of toppings.

1 serving contains:

Cal	Prot	Fat	Carb	Fiber	Chol	Sodium
314	11.7 g	6.7 g	50.5 g	1.6 g	4.8 mg	411 mg

Apple Pancakes: Top pancakes with thin slices of unpeeled apple before turning. *Blueberry Pancakes:* Add 1 cup fresh blueberries and 1 tablespoon brown sugar to batter. *Corn Pancakes:* Fold in 1 cup whole-kernel corn. *Cornmeal Pancakes:* Use 1 cup cornmeal and 1 cup unbleached flour, instead of 2 cups unbleached flour. *Oatmeal Pancakes:* Use 1/2 cup rolled oats, 1 1/2 cups unbleached flour instead of 2 cups unbleached flour. *Raisin Pancakes:* Add 1/2 cup raisins to batter. *Whole Wheat Pancakes:* Use 1 cup whole wheat flour and 1 cup unbleached flour instead of 2 cups unbleached flour.

Basic Crepes

The most unusual and best way you've ever made crepes!

Utensil: Small skillet
Yield: 18 crepes

1	cup all-purpose flour
	dash of salt
3	eggs or ³/₄ cup *egg substitute
¹/₄	cup water
1	cup 2% or *skim milk
1	tablespoon margarine, melted
	vegetable spray

In bowl combine flour and salt; add eggs one at a time; beating well after each addition. Gradually stir in water, milk and margarine; mix well. Cover bowl; let batter set 1-2 hours at room temperature. Flour will expand and thicken batter.

Spray bottom (underside) of skillet with vegetable spray. Preheat skillet, bottom (underside) up, over medium-high heat 3-5 minutes or until a drop of water sizzles off surface.

Pour batter into large dinner plate to a depth of ³/₄". Hold skillet in level position; dip into batter so bottom (underside) is covered. Lift skillet; turn batter side up. Swirl so excess batter fills in any holes or spaces. Place skillet, bottom side up, on the burner. Cook over medium heat until golden brown around edge. Using spatula or tongs, remove crepe from pan bottom; place browned side down on plate. To keep crepes moist, cover immediately. Repeat until all batter is used. If needed, lightly spray bottom of skillet with vegetable spray as sticking occurs.

● ●

1 serving contains:

Cal	Prot	Fat	Carb	Fiber	Chol	Sodium
49.7	2.3 g	1.8 g	5.9 g	0.2 g	0.4 mg	50.4 mg

● ●

Filling for Seafood Crepes

Yield: Filling for 12 crepes

2	(6-ounce) packages frozen crabmeat; flaked
1/2	cup thinly sliced celery
3	tablespoons sliced green onions
1	(8-ounce) can water chestnuts, drained and diced
1	(6-ounce) package frozen cocktail shrimp, divided
1/2	cup reduced-fat or *fat-free mayonnaise
2	tablespoons 2% or *skim milk
3	tablespoons chili sauce
1/2	teaspoon Worcestershire sauce
1	teaspoon onion powder
12	crepes (This recipe can be found on page 5-10)

In medium bowl, combine crabmeat, celery, onions, water chestnuts and one-half of shrimp. Cover; chill 1 hour.

In a large bowl combine mayonnaise, milk, chili sauce, Worcestershire sauce and onion powder; mix thoroughly. Gently stir in remaining shrimp. Cover; chill 1 hour.

Place crepes, browned side down, on waxed paper. Spoon 2 tablespoons crabmeat filling in middle of each crepe; fold crepes in thirds. Arrange on serving dish; spoon sauce over crepes.

• •

1 serving contains:

Cal	Prot	Fat	Carb	Fiber	Chol	Sodium
115.3	11.6 g	2.4 g	12.3 g	0.9 g	53.3 mg	331.4 mg

• •

Filling Idea: Cut leftover baked or boiled potatoes into cubes and beat throughly. Fill crepes along with generous spoonful of Mexican salsa. If desired, add a sprinkling of reduced fat mozzarella cheese and a few leaves of fresh cilantro or parsley (see pg. 1-20 for recipe).

Breakfast Crepes

Utensils: Large skillet, High dome cover; Saladmaster Machine
Yield: Filling for 8 crepes

2	ounces reduced-fat or *fat-free cheddar cheese
	vegetable spray (or margarine, if desired)
8	eggs or 2 cups *egg substitute
$1/2$	cup 2% or *skim milk
1	cup diced Canadian bacon or ham
8	crepes (This recipe can be found on page 5-10)

Process cheese using #1 cone.

Preheat oven to 325 degrees.

Preheat skillet over medium heat; spray with vegetable spray. In a large bowl, beat together eggs and milk. When skillet is hot pour eggs into skillet; stir in Canadian bacon. Cook over medium heat, stirring occasionally, until eggs are set.

Place crepes, browned side down, on waxed paper. Place about $1/3$ cup egg mixture in center of each crepe; top with 1 teaspoon cheese. Fold crepes in thirds; place in high dome cover. Sprinkle remaining cheese over crepes. Bake in preheated oven 10-15 minutes at 325 degrees.

● ●

1 serving contains:

Cal	Prot	Fat	Carb	Fiber	Chol	Sodium
212.7	18.7 g	10.9 g	9.2 g	0.2 g	19.2 mg	662.4 mg

● ●

Filling Idea: Spray a skillet with nonstick spray and heat over medium heat. Add thin slices of apple and cover. Cook until Vapo-Valve clicks. Reduce heat to low and cook 5 minutes or until apple slices are tender. Season to taste with cinnamon and brown sugar. Shortcut idea! Heat prepared apple pie filling and use to fill crepes.

English Muffins

Utensil: Large skillet
Yield: 18-20 muffins

1	cup lukewarm water
2/3	cup scalded 2% or *skim milk
2	teaspoons sugar
1	package active dry yeast
4	cups unbleached flour
3	tablespoons softened margarine
1/2	teaspoon salt
	vegetable spray (or margarine, if desired)

Combine water, milk, and sugar in large bowl. When mixture feels quite hot, but not too hot to touch (about 105-115 degrees), stir in yeast. When mixture bubbles, after about 5 minutes, gradually beat 2 cups flour gradually into milk mixture using wooden spoon.

Cover bowl with cloth. Allow to rise in warm place (about 85 degrees) for 1 1/2 hours, or until dough collapses back into bowl. Beat in margarine and salt. Continue to beat in remaining flour, and knead in flour as dough becomes harder to work.

Place dough on floured board. Pat or press to 1/2-inch thickness. Cut into 3-inch rounds, place on lightly sprayed cookie sheets. Knead scraps, roll or press out dough, and continue to cut into rounds until dough is used up. Let muffin dough stand until it has doubled in bulk.

Preheat skillet over medium heat, spray skillet with vegetable spray. Carefully transfer muffins, one at a time, to skillet using pancake turner. Turn heat to low and cook uncovered until muffins are lightly browned, about 10 minutes. Turn and brown remaining side about 10 minutes. Turn heat slightly higher if muffins do not brown.

To serve, cool slightly. Split muffins horizontally, using 2 forks. Toast and use your favorite spread, if desired.

● ●

1 serving contains:

Cal	Prot	Fat	Carb	Fiber	Chol	Sodium
104	2.8 g	2 g	18.5 g	0.7 g	0.1 mg	81.1 mg

● ●

Whole Wheat Biscuits

Great biscuits, and you don't even heat up the oven!

Utensil: Electric skillet
Yield: 12 biscuits

1	cup whole wheat flour
1	cup all-purpose flour
1	tablespoon baking powder
$1/2$	teaspoon salt
$3/4$	cup 2% or *skim milk
$1/4$	cup canola oil
	vegetable spray

In a medium bowl combine flours, baking powder and salt; stir well. Add milk and oil; stir to form soft dough.

Place dough onto lightly floured surface; knead lightly 2-3 times. Roll dough to $1/2$" thickness; cut with biscuit cutter.

Preheat skillet at 375 degrees, spray with vegetable spray. Place cut biscuits into skillet. Reduce heat to 350 degrees; bake uncovered 5-8 minutes or until golden brown. Turn; continue to cook 5-8 minutes or until brown on other side.

• •

1 serving contains:

Cal	Prot	Fat	Carb	Fiber	Chol	Sodium
116	2.9 g	4.9 g	15.6 g	1.5 g	0.3 mg	126 mg

• •

Shortcut: To use refrigerated biscuits, follow cooking instructions for Whole Wheat Biscuits using electric skillet.

Tip

For lighter biscuits, use unbleached all-purpose flour instead of whole wheat. Unbleached flour has not been treated with chemicals to make it white. Light golden in color, it can be used to replace all-purpose flour in any recipe.

Corn Bread

Utensil: Small skillet
Yield: 8 servings

1	cup yellow cornmeal
3/4	cup all-purpose flour
2	teaspoons baking powder
1/4	teaspoon baking soda
1/2	teaspoon salt
1	cup buttermilk
2	teaspoons margarine
	dash of paprika

In a medium bowl combine cornmeal, flour, baking powder, soda and salt. Melt margarine in skillet over medium heat; pour buttermilk and margarine into dry ingredients (reserving enough margarine to coat skillet); stir just until mixed. Pour into skillet; sprinkle with paprika.

Turn heat to low, cover and cook 15-20 minutes until baked through. To serve from skillet, cut corn bread with plastic knife.

• •

1 serving contains:

Cal	Prot	Fat	Carb	Fiber	Chol	Sodium
117	3.4 g	1.9 g	21.7 g	1.9 g	1.1 mg	292 mg

• •

Shortcut: To use a prepared mix, make batter according to package instructions. Pour into skillet preheated on low and "bake" 15-20 minutes. Sprinkling with paprika adds color.

Other corn bread add-ins:
- cooked, crumbed sausage
- chopped green onion
- chopped red and green bell pepper
- finely chopped jalapeno pepper
- grated fat-free or reduced-fat cheese, cheddar or Monterey jack
- chopped, well-drained salad olives or black olives
- Stir ingredients into batter before baking.

Oatmeal Raisin Scones

A traditional tea bread of England.

Utensil: Large skillet
Yield: 4 servings

1	cup rolled oats, divided
1	cup unbleached flour
2	tablespoons sugar
1 $^1/_2$	teaspoons baking powder
$^1/_4$	teaspoon baking soda
$^1/_8$	teaspoon salt
3	tablespoons margarine, cut into $^1/_2$-inch pieces
$^1/_3$	cup raisins
$^1/_2$-$^3/_4$	cup buttermilk

Grind $^1/_2$ cup of the oats in blender. Place in medium bowl with remaining oats, flour, sugar, baking powder, baking soda, and salt. Add margarine and cut into dry ingredients with pastry blender until the mixture resembles coarse meal. Mix in raisins.

Make a well in center of dry ingredients. Gradually stir in enough buttermilk to make firm, moist dough. Gently knead dough on lightly floured surface until smooth. Divide dough into 4 pieces; form each into thick rounds about 4 inches across.

Heat large skillet over medium heat for 2-3 minutes. When drops of water dance when sprinkled in pan, lightly spray with vegetable spray. Place scones in skillet and turn heat to low. Cover and cook for 15 minutes, then turn, pressing down with spatula to flatten scones. Bake an additional 10-15 minutes, covered, or until golden brown.

1 serving contains:

Cal	Prot	Fat	Carb	Fiber	Chol	Sodium
344	8.3 g	10.6 g	55.1 g	3.8 g	1.7 mg	407 mg

Cheese & Vegetable Corn Bread

Utensils: Small skillet, Saladmaster Machine
Yield: 8 servings

1	ounce reduced-fat or *fat-free cheddar cheese
1	tablespoon chopped onion
1	cup all-purpose flour
1/2	cup white cornmeal
1	tablespoon sugar
1	tablespoon baking powder
2	teaspoons margarine
3/4	cup 2% or *skim milk
1	egg white, beaten
3	tablespoons green pepper, chopped

Process cheese using #1 cone, onion using #2 cone.

In a medium bowl combine flour, cornmeal, sugar and baking powder. Melt margarine in skillet on medium heat. Gradually add milk and egg white, mix well. Add cheese, onion, green pepper and margarine (reserving enough margarine to coat skillet); stir gently to mix.

Pour batter into skillet, turn heat to low, cover; cook 25 minutes. To serve from skillet, cut into squares with plastic knife.

• •

1 serving contains:

Cal	Prot	Fat	Carb	Fiber	Chol	Sodium
117	4.6 g	1.3 g	21.1 g	1.1 g	1 mg	181 mg

• •

Mediterranean touch

Substitute chopped sun-dried tomatoes and black olives for onion and green pepper. If desired, eliminate cheddar cheese and add crumbled Greek feta cheese or blue cheese.

Spanish Corn Bread

Utensils: Electric skillet, Saladmaster Machine
Yield: 10 servings

2	**ounces reduced-fat or *fat-free cheddar cheese**
	vegetable spray
1	**cup cornmeal**
1/2	**teaspoon baking soda**
1/2	**teaspoon salt**
1	**cup canned cream-style corn**
2/3	**cup buttermilk**
1	**4-ounce can green chilies, chopped and drained**
2	**egg whites, slightly beaten**
1	**teaspoon canola oil**

Process cheese using #1 cone.

Preheat electric skillet at 375 degrees, spray lightly with vegetable spray.

In a medium bowl combine cornmeal, baking soda and salt; add corn, buttermilk, chilies, egg whites and oil; mix well.

Spoon one-half of batter into hot skillet; sprinkle with cheese. Add remaining batter. Reduce heat to 250 degrees, cover and cook 12 minutes.

• •

1 serving contains:

Cal	Prot	Fat	Carb	Fiber	Chol	Sodium
89.4	4.7 g	1.2 g	16.2 g	1.8 g	1.6 mg	294 mg

• •

Flavors from around the world:
- **Instead of cheddar, use shredded mozzarella cheese.**
- **Instead of chilies, use 1/2 cup chopped sundried tomatoes or red peppers.**
- **To make it hotter, add 2 teaspoons chopped jalapeno pepper. If green chilies are too hot, substitute 1/2 cup chopped green pepper.**

Pork Chops
with Vegetables

Meats

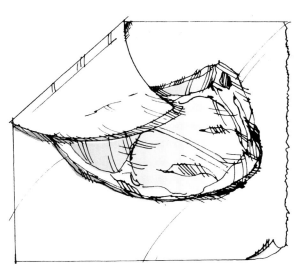

Cooking meats the stove-top, Saladmaster way can enhance flavors, especially of economical cuts; eliminate the need for added fat; save energy and reduce cooking time. At a time when some health-conscious eaters are eliminating all red meat from their diets, the techniques found in this chapter may ease your conscience and allow you to indulge your fondness for meat a couple of times per week, without guilt.

Some guidelines for reducing the fat in beef, lamb, pork or other red meat: trim visible fat, add little or no additional fat, sear the meat to get a "roasted" flavor.

Also consider using wild game such as venison if available. Some persons limit their red meat consumption to venison because it is low in fat and cholesterol. Venison can be used in most of the recipes for beef and, in some cases, pork.

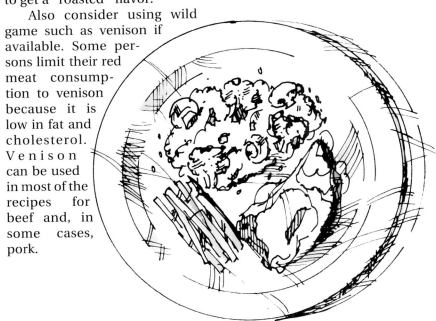

How to cook meat

There are three basic methods for cooking meat on top of the stove: stove-top roasting, pan-broiling (the electric skillet is particularly handy for this), and braising.

1. **Stove-top roasting:** Use this technique for more tender cuts that you might otherwise roast in the oven.
How-to: Preheat Dutch oven 3 to 5 minutes over medium-high heat. (To tell when a pan is properly preheated, splash a few drops of water on the surface. If the drops bead and dance, the pan is ready to use.) Place meat in uncovered pan, pressing down to assure even "searing." Sear meat on all sides until brown. Meat may stick, but will loosen as browning continues. Do not add liquid (unless recipe specifies). Cover; when Vapo-Valve clicks, turn heat to low and cook according to the chart.

Meat	Minutes per pound
Beef	
rare	10
medium rare	12
medium	15
well-done	20
Lamb, leg	
rare	20
medium	25
well-done	30
Pork	25 to 30
Veal	20

2. **Pan-broiling:** This technique works well for cutlets, chops and steaks.
How-to: Preheat skillet over medium-high heat for 3 to 5 minutes. Or preheat electric skillet (375 degrees to 400 degrees). Add meat and cook on one side until brown. Meat may stick, but will loosen as it browns. Turn and cook until brown on other side. If

desired, cover and cook until Vapo-Valve clicks. Reduce heat to low (275 degrees to 300 degrees on electric skillet) and cook 5 to 10 minutes longer. For steaks, cook over medium heat, with lid ajar, according to the chart.

● ●
Boneless steak (such as ribeye)   **Cooking time**

1-inch thick
  Rare (red) . . . . .4 minutes on 1 side, 3 minutes other side
  Medium rare (pink) . . . .5 minutes on 1 side, 4 minutes other side
  Medium (no pink) . . . . .6 minutes on 1 side, 5 minutes other side
  Well-done (dry) . . . . . . .7 minutes on 1 side, 6 minutes other side
● ●

3. *Braising:* This method of first browning then cooking in liquid is particularly good for tougher, economical cuts. Be sure to trim fat well.
How-to: Preheat pan (usually skillet or Dutch oven) over medium-high heat for 3 to 5 minutes. (To tell when a pan is properly preheated, splash a few drops of water on the surface. If the drops bead and dance, the pan is ready to use.) Add meat and cook on all sides until brown. Add ¹/4 cup liquid (water, wine, broth, for example) or as required by recipe. Cover; cook until Vapo-Valve clicks, turn heat to low and cook according to the chart.

● ●
Meat   **Minutes per pound**

Beef . . . . .20 to 25
Lamb . . . . .20 to 25
Pork . . . . .25 to 30
Veal . . . . .20 to 25
Venison . . . . .20 to 25
● ●

Skillet Meat Loaf

Another Saladmaster dinner favorite, for decades. Start with the basic recipe then change it to suit your taste.

Utensils: Large skillet, Saladmaster Machine
Yield: 8 servings

2	ounces reduced-fat or *fat-free cheddar cheese
1	small onion
1	medium potato
1	(8-ounce) can tomato sauce, divided
2	pounds lean *ground beef or ground turkey
2	eggs or 1/2 cup *egg substitute, slightly beaten
1	teaspoon salt

Process cheese and potato using #1 cone, onion using #2 cone.

Measure 1/3 cup tomato sauce; set aside. In a large bowl mix onion, potato, beef, remaining tomato sauce, eggs and salt. Mix well; shape into loaf, place in skillet; top with reserved tomato sauce. Cover; cook over medium heat until Vapo-Valve clicks, reduce heat to low and cook 30-35 minutes. Sprinkle cheese over meat loaf. Cover; cook 3-4 minutes until cheese melts.

• •

1 serving contains:

Cal	Prot	Fat	Carb	Fiber	Chol	Sodium
363	32.7 g	23.1 g	5.8 g	0.6 g	100 mg	606 mg

• •

Roast with Vegetables

Utensil: Dutch oven
Yield: 6 to 8 servings.

1	(4-pound) pot roast, such as chuck, chuck tender or *rump
1/2	teaspoon *garlic powder or granulated garlic (may use 1 to 2 fresh garlic cloves, finely chopped)
5	carrots, peeled and cut in 3-inch lengths
5	potatoes, peeled and cut into quarters
1	large yellow onion, peeled and cut into quarters

Preheat Dutch oven over medium heat. Place roast in Dutch oven. Cook on one side for 10 minutes or until brown and meat loosens in pan. Turn roast and season with garlic powder or granulated garlic and pepper.

Cook 10 minutes longer on other side. Add vegetables (including fresh garlic if using) and cover. When Vapo-Valve clicks, reduce heat to low and cook 1 $^1/_2$ hours or until tender. Season to taste with salt substitute or salt.

1 serving contains:

Cal	Prot	Fat	Carb	Fiber	Chol	Sodium
620	63.3 g	32.2 g	16.7 g	2 g	165 mg	151 mg

Pan juices, meat sauces

Juices left in the pan after stovetop roasting can make wonderful natural or thickened gravies. Simply remove meat from pan and keep warm. Skim off fat in pan, then add a few tablespoons of stock, water or wine and place pan over medium heat. Use a wooden spoon to scrape brown particles from bottom and sides of pan, stirring them into liquid. Cook for a few minutes to reduce the liquid to concentrate flavor or thicken slightly. Season to taste and serve.

When there is substantial liquid, as with a pot roast, you may thicken the juices with cornstarch, arrowroot or flour. Skim off any fat. If time allows, refrigerate overnight and remove any fat that congeals. A few ice cubes placed in a warm liquid will also attract congealed fat. Remove quickly with slotted spoon. An absorbent paper towel also can be used to soak up fat around the edges of a pan.

1 tablespoon cornstarch thickens 1 $^1/_2$ to 2 cups liquid.
2 $^1/_2$ teaspoons arrowroot thickens 1 cup liquid.

Cornstarch and arrowroot do not cloud sauces but they lose their thickening power when reheated or if overheated. For the most stable thickener, use flour.

2 to 3 tablespoons flour thickens 1 $^1/_2$ to 2 cups liquid.

Combine flour with double the amount of water and stir to make a smooth paste. Stir or whisk into warm liquid to prevent lumping. Heat until thickened.

Instant dissolving flour may be used by sprinkling directly into liquid; stir or whisk to prevent lumping.

Beef-Stuffed Peppers

Utensils: Large skillet, Saladmaster Machine
Yield: 4 servings

1	**small carrot**
4	**large *green or red peppers**
1	**medium onion**
1	**celery stalk**
1	**clove garlic, minced**
3/4	**pound lean *ground beef or ground turkey**
3/4	**cup cooked rice**
1/4	**cup fresh parsley minced**
1	**teaspoon soy sauce**
1/2	**teaspoon dried marjoram, finely crumbled**
	dash of freshly grated nutmeg
1	**cup tomato sauce**
1	**tablespoon water**

Choose peppers with flat bottoms, so they stand upright. Cut off pepper tops, remove seeds, set aside.

Process carrot using #1 cone, onion, celery and pepper tops using #2 cone.

Place peppers upside down in large skillet. Add 1 tablespoon water, cover; cook over medium heat until Vapo-Valve clicks, reduce heat to low and cook 3-4 minutes.

Remove peppers, drain upside down on paper towel, set aside.

Combine the carrot, onion, celery, pepper tops, and beef in skillet with any remaining liquid. Cover; cook over medium heat until Vapo-Valve clicks, reduce heat to low and cook 10 minutes. Stir in rice, parsley, soy sauce, marjoram, nutmeg, and 1/4 cup of tomato sauce, stir. Cover, cook over low heat for 5 minutes.

Place peppers upright, spoon stuffing into peppers. Spoon 1/2 of remaining tomato sauce into bottom of skillet. Place peppers upright in skillet, spooning remaining tomato sauce over each pepper.

Cover; cook over medium heat until Vapo-Valve clicks, reduce heat to low and cook 20 minutes. Serve peppers with tomato sauce on the side.

• •

1 serving contains:

Cal	Prot	Fat	Carb	Fiber	Chol	Sodium
339	24.2 g	16.5 g	24.5 g	3.5 g	74 mg	541 mg

• •

Zucchini and Beef Parmesan

Utensils: Electric skillet, Saladmaster Machine
Yields: 6-8 servings

1	ounce fresh Parmesan cheese
2	ounces reduced-fat or *fat-free Cheddar cheese
2	small onions
1	medium green pepper, chopped
4	small zucchini
1	pound lean *ground beef or ground turkey
1	(16-ounce) can chopped tomatoes, drained
1	(8-ounce) can tomato sauce
1	(6-ounce) can tomato paste
1/2	teaspoon dried oregano
1/4	teaspoon garlic powder
1/4	teaspoon black pepper

Process cheeses using #1 cone, onions using #2 cone, zucchini and green pepper using #3 cone.

Place meat and onions in electric skillet, cover; cook at 325 degrees, stirring occasionally until meat is browned and onion is tender.

Add tomatoes, tomato sauce, tomato paste and green pepper. Cover; cook at 325 degrees until Vapo-Valve clicks, reduce heat to low and cook 15 minutes.

Stir in Cheddar cheese, oregano, garlic powder and black pepper. Add zucchini. Cover; simmer 10 minutes. Sprinkle with Parmesan cheese. Cover; simmer 10 minutes.

• •
1 serving contains:

Cal	Prot	Fat	Carb	Fiber	Chol	Sodium
238	20.6 g	4.8 g	13.8 g	3.3 g	53 mg	585 mg

• •

Electric Skillet Lasagna

Utensils: Electric skillet, Saladmaster Machine, 3-quart saucepan, Steamer Inset
Yields: 8-10 servings

12	ounces reduced-fat or fat-free mozzarella cheese
4	cups water
2	pounds lean ground beef or ground turkey
1	teaspoon garlic powder

Electric Skillet Lasagna, Cont.

1	teaspoon celery salt
1	(1-ounce) package Italian dry seasoning
1	(6-ounce) can tomato paste
1	(16-ounce) can tomato sauce
16	ounces fat-free cottage cheese
1	(8-ounce) box uncooked lasagna noodles

Process cheese using #2 cone.

Pour water into saucepan; bring to boil over medium heat. Place ground beef in steamer; insert into saucepan. Cover; steam 6 minutes.

In bowl add beef, garlic powder, celery salt, Italian seasoning, tomato paste and tomato sauce; mix well.

In cold electric skillet layer in the following order:

- $1/2$ meat sauce mixture
- $1/2$ uncooked noodles
- $1/2$ cottage cheese
- $1/2$ mozzarella
- remaining meat sauce
- remaining lasagna noodles
- remaining cottage cheese
- remaining mozzarella

Cover; cook 25-30 minutes at 225 degrees. Turn control off and let stand 10 minutes or until set.

1 serving contains:

Cal	Prot	Fat	Carb	Fiber	Chol	Sodium
444	43.8 g	17.9 g	27.9 g	2.7 g	87.1 mg	1008 mg

Shipwreck

A one-pan meal all in itself. A long-time Saladmaster favorite.

Utensils: Large skillet, Saladmaster Machine
Yields: 6 servings

1	small onion
4	medium potatoes
2	pounds lean *ground beef or ground turkey
$1/2$	cup uncooked rice
1	(15-ounce) can kidney beans, slightly drained

1   teaspoon Italian Seasoning
1   (8-ounce) can tomato sauce

Process onion using #2 cone, potatoes using #4 cone.
 Layer in the following order:
 Brown beef in skillet, add onion and potatoes. Sprinkle rice around outer edge of skillet. Spoon beans over rice, sprinkle Italian seasoning, then pour tomato sauce over all. Cover; cook over medium heat until Vapo-Valve clicks, reduce heat to low and cook 35-40 minutes.

1 serving contains:

Cal	Prot	Fat	Carb	Fiber	Chol	Sodium
593	44.2 g	29 g	38.8 g	6.6 g	132 mg	589 mg

Applesauce Pork Chops

Utensil: Electric skillet
Yield: 6 servings

6   pork chops
1 1/2 cups applesauce
       dash cinnamon
       cornstarch

Preheat electric skillet at 375 degrees. Add pork chops; brown both sides. Place 1/4 cup applesauce on each pork chop, sprinkle with cinnamon. Cover; cook until Vapo-Valve clicks, reduce heat to 225 degrees and cook 20 minutes or until chops are tender. Remove pork chops. Slowly stir in cornstarch to thicken remaining meat juice; serve over chops.

1 serving contains:

Cal	Prot	Fat	Carb	Fiber	Chol	Sodium
431	33.4 g	29.1 g	6.9 g	1 g	0 mg	69.3 mg

Beef Stroganoff

Utensil: Large skillet, Saladmaster Machine
Yield: 4 servings

1 1/2	**small onions**
2	**pounds lean sirloin, thinly sliced on diagonal**
1 1/2	**cups mushrooms, quartered**
1/4	**cup *sherry or beef stock**
1	**cup fat-free sour cream**
1/2	**teaspoon Dijon-style mustard**
1/4	**teaspoon salt**
	dash of freshly ground black pepper
1/4	**cup fresh parsley, minced, garnish**

Process onions using #4 cone.

Preheat large skillet over medium heat for 5 minutes. Add meat in one layer, brown on both sides and remove from pan, set aside. Meat should just be cooked through. Add onions to hot pan and stir for 2-3 minutes, browning slightly. Add mushrooms and sherry or beef stock. Cover; cook over medium heat until Vapo-Valve clicks, reduce heat to low and cook 15 minutes, until onions and mushrooms are quite tender. Remove lid, return heat to medium, and boil down liquid in vegetables until reduced by half.

In a small bowl combine sour cream, mustard, salt, and pepper. Add meat to vegetables in pan and stir in sour cream. Heat through.

For an even healthier meal, serve stroganoff over brown rice or whole-grain noodles, sprinkled with parsley.

1 serving contains:

Cal	Prot	Fat	Carb	Fiber	Chol	Sodium
703	65.4 g	43 g	6.3 g	1.2 g	179 mg	330 mg

Oriental Pork Chops

Utensil: Large skillet
Yields: 6 servings

1	**cup orange juice**
1	**tablespoon fresh gingerroot or 1 teaspoon ground *ginger, minced**
3	**cloves garlic, minced**

1/2	teaspoon crushed whole black peppercorns (see note below)
1/4	teaspoon cayenne pepper
2	tablespoons reduced-sodium soy sauce
6	pork chops, 1-inch thick

Combine orange juice, ginger, garlic, crushed black pepper, cayenne, and soy sauce in shallow container. Place pork chops in marinade, turn once, cover, refrigerate several hours or overnight.

Place pork chops in large skillet and spoon marinade over chops. Cover; cook over medium heat, until Vapo-Valve clicks, reduce heat to low and cook 20 minutes. Serve pork chops and marinade over rice.

• •

1 serving contains:

Cal	Prot	Fat	Carb	Fiber	Chol	Sodium
430	34.2 g	29.2 g	5.5 g	0.2 g	0 mg	228 mg

• •

NOTE: To crush peppercorns, place them between two sheets of waxed paper and crush with a rolling pin or rubber mallet. Do not substitute ground pepper for the crushed peppercorns because dish will be too hot. For healthiest version, serve over brown rice with large green salad.

Spaghetti Sauce with Meat

Utensils: Large skillet, Saladmaster Machine
Yields: 6-8 servings

1	medium carrot
1	medium onion
1/2	medium green or red pepper, diced
1/2	pound lean *ground beef or ground turkey
2	cloves garlic, minced
2	medium tomatoes, seeded and finely chopped
1/2	cup mushrooms, sliced
1/2	teaspoon dried basil
1/2	teaspoon dried oregano
1/4	teaspoon dried thyme
1/4	teaspoon dried marjoram
	dash of freshly ground pepper
6	cups tomato sauce

Spaghetti Sauce with Meat, Cont.

Process carrot using #1 cone, onion and green pepper using #2 cone.

Place meat, carrot, onion, green pepper and garlic in skillet. Cover; cook over medium heat until Vapo-Valve clicks, reduce heat to low and cook 4-5 minutes, until meat is brown.

Stir in chopped tomatoes, mushrooms, basil, oregano, thyme, marjoram, and pepper, and cook until mushrooms have lost their raw appearance, about 2-3 minutes. Add tomato sauce, stir. Cover; when Vapo-Valve clicks reduce heat to low and cook 10-15 minutes. Serve over cooked spaghetti, preferably whole wheat or artichoke varieties.

1 serving contains:

Cal	Prot	Fat	Carb	Fiber	Chol	Sodium
156	10.3 g	4.2 g	18.5 g	4.2 g	24.7 mg	1140 mg

Calf's Liver with Onions

Utensils: Large skillet, Saladmaster Machine
Yield: 4 servings

2	small onions
1	teaspoon olive oil
2	teaspoons margarine
4	slices calf's liver
1/4	cup all-purpose flour
1/4	teaspoon dried thyme
1/4	teaspoon freshly ground black pepper
1/4	teaspoon salt
1/4	cup chicken broth
	fresh parsley, garnish

Process onions using #4 cone.

Heat oil and margarine in large skillet over medium heat, add onions. Cover; when Vapo-Valve clicks reduce heat to low and cook 10-15 minutes, until very tender.

Uncover, stir onions until lightly browned. Remove, set aside. Dredge liver in flour, thyme, pepper, and salt, place in hot skillet. Sauté quickly over medium heat 1-2 minutes on each side, just until liver is pink inside. Spoon onions over liver, add stock, and cook until sauce is slightly thickened, about 1 minute. Serve immediately, garnished with fresh parsley, over brown rice or with whole-grain noodles.

● ●
1 serving contains:

Cal	Prot	Fat	Carb	Fiber	Chol	Sodium
111	6.9 g	4.6 g	10.3 g	0.9 g	0.1 mg	227 mg

● ●

Oriental Pepper Steak

Utensils: Wok, Saladmaster Machine;
Yield: 6 servings

1	**medium onion**
3	**small green peppers**
1 $^1/_2$	**pounds lean round steak, cut into thin strips**
2	**tablespoons Worcestershire sauce**
2	**tablespoons reduced-sodium soy sauce**
1 $^1/_2$	**cups water**
1	**tablespoon flour**
1	**(16-ounce) can whole tomatoes, peeled and cut in chunks**

Process onion using #1 cone, green peppers using #4 cone.

Preheat wok on medium-high; add onion and meat. Sauté until meat is slightly brown. Reduce heat to medium, add Worcestershire sauce, soy sauce and water. Cover; cook until Vapo-Valve clicks, reduce heat to low and cook 20 minutes.

Add green pepper; cook 10 minutes. Add enough water to flour to make a thin paste, add to skillet, stir in tomatoes; cook 10 minutes.

Serve over cooked brown rice.

● ●
1 serving contains:

Cal	Prot	Fat	Carb	Fiber	Chol	Sodium
353	30.8 g	21 g	9.1 g	1.6 g	94.7 mg	401 mg

● ●

Spice it up

When sauce thickens, remove from heat. Add in 2 to 3 tablespoons fat-free sour cream and 1 teaspoon prepared horseradish or to taste. Serve over chops.

Stuff

Utensil: Electric skillet, Saladmaster Machine
Yield: 6-8 servings

1	**medium onion**
2	**large potatoes**
1/4	**medium head cabbage**
2	**carrots**
1	**pound extra lean *beef or turkey, ground**
1	**teaspoon Worcestershire sauce**
1/8	**teaspoon freshly ground black pepper**
1	**can low-fat, low-sodium cream of chicken soup**
6	**slices fat-free American cheese**

Process onion, potatoes, cabbage and carrots using #2 cone.

Brown ground beef in skillet, drain. Remove 1/4 of the ground beef, set aside. Layer vegetables in order listed over ground beef, drizzle Worcestershire sauce over all then sprinkle with black pepper. Crumble remainder of ground beef over vegetables. Spread soup over this.

Set skillet to 325 degrees, cover; when Vapo-Valve clicks, reduce heat to 225 degrees and cook 15 minutes or until vegetables are tender. Turn control off, add cheese slices, cover and let sit 5 minutes.

● ●

1 serving contains:

Cal	Prot	Fat	Carb	Fiber	Chol	Sodium
229	17.8 g	11.5 g	13.1 g	1.3 g	52.5 mg	344 mg

● ●

Pork Tenderloin Diane

Utensil: Large skillet
Yield: 5 servings

1	**pound pork tenderloin, cut crosswise into 10 pieces**
2	**teaspoons lemon pepper**
2	**tablespoons margarine**
2	**tablespoons lemon juice**
1	**tablespoon Worcestershire sauce**
1	**teaspoon Dijon-style mustard**
1	**tablespoon finely chopped chives or parsley**
	whole chives (garnish)

Press each tenderloin piece into 1-inch-thick medallion; sprinkle surfaces with lemon pepper. Melt margarine in large skillet over medium heat. Add medallions; cook 7-8 minutes on each side. Remove pork to serving platter; keep warm. Stir lemon juice, Worcestershire sauce and mustard into pan juices in skillet. Cook, stirring, until heated through. Pour sauce over medallions; sprinkle with chopped chives. Garnish with whole chives.

● ●

1 serving contains:

Cal	Prot	Fat	Carb	Fiber	Chol	Sodium
373	26.8 g	28 g	1.55 g	.06 g	0 mg	495 mg

● ●

When thawing meat, and time allows, place in the refrigerator overnight. For faster thawing, defrost in the microwave according to manufacturer's directions or place in cold water, changing water frequently. Do not thaw meat on countertop at room temperature for extended periods of time.

It is, however, a good idea to let meat come to room temperature before cooking. With a roast, remove from refrigerator thirty minutes to an hour before cooking, when time allows.

Meat may be stored up to four days in the refrigerator. Ground meat should be refrigerated no longer than two days; freeze for longer storage. Recent food poisoning episodes have underscored the need to cook ground beef to at least medium doneness. Solid pieces of meat can still be enjoyed rare or medium rare.

Remember to refrigerate meat when marinating. Do not brush reserved marinade on cooked meat or use for sauce without bringing it to a boil. This eliminates the chance of bacterial contamination from raw to cooked meat.

Sweet and Sour Pork

Utensil: Large skillet
Yield: 6 servings

1	**grapefruit**
1 1/4	**pounds boneless pork tenderloin, trimmed of all fat**
1/3	**cup grapefruit juice**
2	**tablespoons low-sodium soy sauce**
1	**clove garlic, minced**
2	**teaspoons light brown sugar, divided**
2	**tablespoons cornstarch**
1	**tablespoon vegetable oil**
2	**teaspoons minced gingerroot**
8	**green onions, cut into 2-inch pieces**
1	**medium red or green pepper, cut into 1-inch cubes**
1/4	**cup ketchup**
1/3	**cup low-fat, low sodium chicken broth**

Peel grapefruit and carefully remove white pith. Carefully section grapefruit with paring knife, peeling fruit away from membrane. Set aside.

Cut pork into 1-inch cubes. In a medium bowl combine grapefruit juice, soy sauce, garlic and 1 teaspoon brown sugar, stir until blended. Add pork; stir. Cover and refrigerate 30 minutes. Remove pork from marinade with slotted spoon, reserving marinade. Place cornstarch in shallow dish; add pork. Toss until lightly coated.

Heat oil in large skillet over medium-high heat until hot, but not smoking. Add pork and cook on all sides, about 7 to 10 minutes until golden brown. Remove pork to warm plate. Add ginger, scallions and red pepper to skillet. Cook and stir 2 to 3 minutes until scallions are slightly limp. Add ketchup, chicken broth, remaining 1 teaspoon brown sugar and reserved marinade. Bring to a boil over medium-high heat. Add browned pork and grapefruit sections; cook about 1 to 2 minutes until pork is no longer pink and sauce has thickened slightly. Serve immediately.

● ●

1 serving contains:

Cal	Prot	Fat	Carb	Fiber	Chol	Sodium
421	29.3 g	26.6 g	15.1 g	1.3 g	.04 mg	343 mg

● ●

Sweet and Sour Shrimp

Seafood

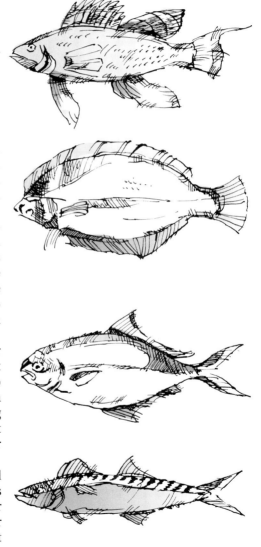

Fish and other seafoods have gotten much attention in recent years. Because fish is naturally low in fat, it is a smart choice for those interested in a healthful eating plan. While many cooks have known that fish is a smart addition to a family's menu, they have been reluctant to prepare it often. Fish has a reputation of being difficult to cook. Frying is the most familiar method of preparation, but it is not a good choice for those concerned about fat in the diet.

Even though it is low in fat, fish can become an indulgent dish if it is breaded and fried or smothered in a rich cream or cheese sauce.

Our cooking methods make it easy to prepare fish in tasteful, imaginative ways without deep-frying or the addition of rich sauces. The most important thing to remember when cooking fish is not to overcook it.

Appearance is another clue. Fish is done when it turns from translucent to white. For those who like it a little more cooked, try flaking with a fork. It is well done at that point and will suffer from further cooking.

Shellfish like shrimp and scallops cook very quickly. As soon as they lose their translucence and appear firm, remove from heat immediately.

Meaty fish like tuna can be served rare to medium rare for those who like the taste of impeccably fresh fish lightly cooked.

The omega-3 bonus

One of the most significant nutritional benefits of fish is the discovery in recent years of special oils in some fish that are thought to help prevent heart disease. Called omega-3 fatty acids, these fish oils are thought to help lower blood cholesterol and reduce the risk of dangerous blood clots.

In general, the fish with the most omega-3s are those that swim in deep, cold waters, including: tuna, salmon, trout, sardines, swordfish, herring and mackerel. Salmon, tuna and swordfish have grown in popularity in recent years because they are firm-fleshed enough to stand up to outdoor cooking on the grill. Our techniques make it possible to enjoy those fish prepared indoors on the stovetop as well.

Tuna Steaks with Honey-Scallion Marinade

Utensil: Large skillet
Yield: 4 servings

4	tuna steaks
1/4	cup sliced scallions (white portions only)
1	tablespoon olive oil
1	tablespoon lemon juice
1	tablespoon reduced-sodium soy sauce
1	tablespoon honey
2	tablespoons green scallion tops, diagonally sliced, garnish

Place fish in skillet. Combine white portion of scallions, oil, lemon juice, soy sauce, and honey in food processor or blender, process until smooth. Pour over fish, marinate 20-30 minutes in the refrigerator, turning after 10 minutes.

Cover skillet; cook over medium heat until Vapo-Valve clicks, reduce heat to low and cook 12-15 minutes or until fish flakes easily. Time will vary according to thickness of fish. Sprinkle with sliced scallion greens.

1 serving contains:

Cal	Prot	Fat	Carb	Fiber	Chol	Sodium
178	11.8 g	9.4 g	11.5 g	0.2 g	26.6 mg	208 mg

Haddock with Garden Vegetables

Utensils: Large skillet, Saladmaster Machine
Yield: 4 servings

1	**small zucchini**
1	**small yellow squash**
3	**green onions, thinly sliced**
1	**sweet Italian frying pepper or** ¹/2 **red or *green pepper, cut in 2-inch strips**
2	**cups cherry tomatoes, halved, or *chopped tomatoes**
6	**basil leaves, minced, or** ¹/2 **teaspoon *dried basil**
1	**tablespoon fresh parsley, minced**
	dash of freshly ground black pepper
1	**pound haddock fillets, cut in serving pieces**

Process zucchini and squash using #4 cone.

Place zucchini, squash, green onion, pepper strips, tomatoes, basil, parsley, and dash of pepper in skillet, stir.

Cover; cook over medium heat until Vapo-Valve clicks, reduce heat to low and cook 15 minutes.

Place fish in pan, spooning vegetables over each. Cover and continue to cook over low heat 8-10 minutes, or just until fish flakes easily. Serve hot over cooked brown rice.

● ●

1 serving contains:

Cal	Prot	Fat	Carb	Fiber	Chol	Sodium
128	22.9 g	1.2 g	8.8 g	2.8 g	64.6 mg	88.2 mg

● ●

Marinated Sole with Fresh Tomato-Coriander Sauce

Utensil: Small skillet
Yield: 2 servings

4	**sole fillets**
¹/4	**cup lime juice**
2	**tablespoons dry vermouth or *lemon juice**
1	**teaspoon olive oil**
2	**cloves garlic, minced**
1	**tomato, chopped**
1	**tablespoon fresh coriander leaves, minced**
	dash of freshly ground black pepper

Marinated Sole with Fresh Tomato-Coriander Sauce, Cont.

Place fish in a shallow dish. In a small bowl combine lime juice and vermouth, pour over fish. Marinate 15-30 minutes in refrigerator, turning after 10 minutes.

Place skillet over medium heat, add oil and garlic. Stir about 1 minute, add chopped tomato, coriander, and black pepper. Cover; cook over medium heat until Vapo-Valve clicks, reduce heat to low and cook 10 minutes. Remove cover and mash tomatoes with back of spoon.

Drain fish reserving 2 tablespoons of marinade. Stir reserved marinade into tomato mixture and arrange fish over top of sauce. Cover; cook over low heat 10-12 minutes, or until fish flakes easily. Carefully remove fish to serving plate. Spoon tomato-coriander sauce over fish and serve with cooked brown rice.

1 serving contains:

Cal	Prot	Fat	Carb	Fiber	Chol	Sodium
465	86.4 g	8 g	8.4 g	1.2 g	218 mg	376 mg

How long to cook fish: Cook fish—fillets, steaks or whole—10 minutes for every inch of thickness. Measure at the thickest part. A $3/4$-inch thick fillet requires about 7 to 8 minutes of cooking. A 1 $1/2$-inch thick whole trout will be done in about 12 to 15 minutes.

Bluefish and Green Onions

Although the term bluefish describes any type of fish that is blue, there is an actual bluefish. The predatory fish is found in the Atlantic and Indian Oceans, and is prized as a sport fish and harvested as a valuable food fish.

Utensil: Large skillet
Yield: 2 servings

$3/4$	pound thick bluefish fillet
1	tablespoon reduced-sodium soy sauce
2	tablespoons dry white wine or *lemon juice
1	tablespoon water
$1/4$	cup green onion, finely chopped
1	tablespoon fresh gingerroot, finely chopped
1	tablespoon fresh parsley, minced

Place fish in skillet, skin side up, add soy sauce, wine, and water. Marinate 20-30 minutes in the refrigerator, turning after 10 minutes. Combine green onion and gingerroot, press onto fish.

Cover; cook over medium heat until Vapo-Valve clicks, reduce heat to low and cook 12-15 minutes or until fish flakes easily. Sprinkle with minced fresh parsley.

1 serving contains:

Cal	Prot	Fat	Carb	Fiber	Chol	Sodium
294	45.6 g	8.6 g	5.3 g	0.5 g	107 mg	373 mg

Salmon Burgers

Utensils: 1-quart saucepan; Large skillet
Yield: 4 servings

1/2	cup cooked brown or *white rice
4	tablespoons lemon juice
1	(16-ounce) can salmon, drained
1	small carrot, cut in chunks
1	small onion, quartered
1/2	teaspoon grated lemon rind
2	teaspoons olive oil
	lemon wedges, garnish
	dill sprigs, garnish

Place cooked rice and lemon juice in saucepan. Cover; cook over medium heat until Vapo-Valve clicks, reduce heat to low and cook 3-4 minutes, just until rice is quite soft.

Meanwhile, place fish in mixing bowl, remove skin; crush bones and combine with fish. Place rice, carrot and onion in food processor or blender, process until smooth. Stir blended rice mixture and lemon rind into salmon until well blended. Shape into 4 patties.

Place oil in skillet, heat over medium heat. When hot add patties.

Cook until browned, about 4-5 minutes, then turn carefully and cook another 4-5 minutes to brown other side.

1 serving contains:

Cal	Prot	Fat	Carb	Fiber	Chol	Sodium
211	21.3 g	9.1 g	10.5 g	1.4 g	68 mg	53 mg

Poached Bay Scallops

Utensil: Large skillet
Yield: 4 servings

1/4	cup dry white wine, fish broth or *lemon juice
1	tablespoon minced shallots or *green onions (white part only)
1	pound bay scallops

Place wine in large skillet with minced shallots. Cover; cook over medium heat until Vapo-Valve clicks. Add scallops, replace lid, when valve clicks, briefly stir. Reduce heat to low and cook 4-5 minutes, or until scallops are tender and look opaque. Drain.
    Serve hot over rice.
    To serve chilled, cool scallops, toss with Cucumber-Dill Sauce, refrigerate to chill. Serve on a bed of lettuce or in scallop shells (serves 6 as an appetizer).

NOTE: Bay scallops are small, nutty, and sweet. Calico "scallops," pressed from firm-fleshed fish, are not true scallops, but are less expensive and can be substituted. If using the larger sea scallops, quarter them.

1 serving contains:

Cal	Prot	Fat	Carb	Fiber	Chol	Sodium
134	26 g	1.2 g	5.1 g	0.1 g	49.9 mg	224 mg

Lemon-Glazed Salmon Fillets

Utensil: Large skillet
Yield: 4 servings

2	tablespoons margarine
2	tablespoons packed dark brown sugar
2	tablespoons fresh lemon juice
2	pounds red salmon fillets
	lemon slices, garnish
	fresh parsley sprigs, garnish

Melt margarine in skillet over medium heat, stir in brown sugar and lemon juice. Gently place fish in lemon mixture, skin side up. Cover;

when Vapo-Valve clicks, reduce heat to low and cook 8-10 minutes or until fish flakes easily.

Carefully transfer fish to serving platter, placing skin side down. Return heat to medium and boil down sauce until thickened, stirring constantly. Drizzle sauce from pan over fillets. Garnish with lemon slices and parsley sprigs and serve.

1 serving contains:

Cal	Prot	Fat	Carb	Fiber	Chol	Sodium
567	62 g	30.6 g	7.3 g	0.03 g	197 mg	229 mg

Breaded Orange Roughy Fillets

Utensil: Large skillet
Yield: 4 servings

1 1/4-1 1/2 pounds *orange roughy fillets or any white fish
3/4   cup all-purpose flour
1/4   teaspoon freshly ground pepper
1   egg, or 1 *egg white, beaten
1   tablespoon water
1   tablespoon canola oil, divided
1 1/2   cups fresh bread crumbs
         lemon wedges

Score fish and cut into serving size pieces; rinse and pat dry. Combine flour and pepper, dredge fish, shake off any excess flour.

Combine egg, water, and 1 teaspoon oil in a shallow bowl. Dip fish in egg mixture, letting excess drain back into bowl. Roll fish in crumbs until coated. Place fish on plate, cover, and refrigerate 1/2 hour so crumbs adhere to fish.

Heat skillet on medium until drops of water dance when sprinkled in pan. Add 2 teaspoons oil then add fish. Cook 2 minutes on each side, just until fish flakes easily. Serve hot with lemon wedges.

1 serving contains:

Cal	Prot	Fat	Carb	Fiber	Chol	Sodium
623	47.3 g	23.4 g	52.1 g	2.1 g	157 mg	406 mg

Sweet and Sour Shrimp

Utensils: Large skillet, Saladmaster Machine
Yield: 4 servings

2	small carrots
1	medium onion
1/2	red, *green, or yellow pepper
2	stalks broccoli
1 1/2	pounds large shrimp
1	tablespoon canola oil
3	green onions, sliced diagonally

Sauce

3	tablespoons rice wine vinegar
1/4	cup tomato sauce
1/4	cup water
2	tablespoons packed dark brown sugar
2	teaspoons cornstarch
1	teaspoon reduced-sodium soy sauce
2	cloves garlic, minced
1/2	teaspoon fresh ginger or 1/8 teaspoon *ground ginger

Process carrots and onion using #4 cone, red pepper using #5 cone.

Separate broccoli into florets. Peel and devein shrimp. Prepare sauce by combining all sauce ingredients in a small bowl.

Heat skillet over medium heat until drops of water dance when sprinkled in pan. Add oil, carrots and onion; cook 2 minutes, stirring constantly. Add red pepper, green onions, broccoli, and shrimp, stir.

Pour sauce over shrimp mixture. Cover; cook until Vapo-Valve clicks, reduce heat to low, and cook 6-8 minutes, until shrimp are opaque throughout and vegetables are crisp-tender. Serve over rice.

• •

1 serving contains:

Cal	Prot	Fat	Carb	Fiber	Chol	Sodium
290	39 g	5.7 g	21.3 g	4.5 g	332 mg	551 mg

• •

How to store

To keep fish fresh in the refrigerator, place ice in two self-sealing plastic bags. Place one bag on a plate and lay fish, wrapped in plastic, on top. Cover the fish with the second bag of ice. Serve within a day of purchase.

Seafood Salad

A spritly meal, this seafood salad is a meal within itself.

Utensils: 3-quart saucepan, Saladmaster Machine
Yield: 6 servings

1	celery stalk
1/2	pound large shrimp
1	pound *salmon, orange roughy or cod
1/4	cup dry white wine or 2 tablespoons dry white wine + 2 tablespoons *water
2	green onions, thinly sliced
1/4	cup plain, reduced-fat or *fat-free yogurt
2	tablespoons reduced-fat or *fat-free mayonnaise
1	teaspoon Dijon-style mustard
1	teaspoon lime juice
1	teaspoon fresh tarragon, minced
	dash of freshly ground black pepper
	red leaf lettuce, garnish
	cherry tomatoes, garnish
	fresh tarragon sprigs, garnish

Process celery using #2 cone.

Shell and devein shrimp. Place fish, shrimp and wine in pan. Cover; cook over medium heat until Vapo-Valve clicks, reduce heat to low and cook 6-8 minutes, or until shrimp is opaque and fish flakes easily.

Gently lift fish and shrimp from pan, drain and cool. Cut fish into bite-size pieces, removing any bones. Cut shrimp into thirds. In a large bowl combine celery, green onions, yogurt, mayonnaise, mustard, lime juice, tarragon, and pepper. Add shrimp and fish; toss gently.

Line salad bowl or plate with lettuce leaves, spoon salad on top, garnish with cherry tomatoes and tarragon.

● ●

1 serving contains:

Cal	Prot	Fat	Carb	Fiber	Chol	Sodium
140	23.6 g	3.4 g	2.8 g	0.2 g	114 mg	213 mg

● ●

Mako Shark in White Wine

Utensil: Small skillet
Yield: 2 servings

2	mako shark steaks, swordfish or *salmon
2	tablespoons white wine or dry vermouth or *lemon juice
	lemon slices, garnish
	fresh herb sprigs, garnish

Add fish and wine to skillet. Cover; cook over medium heat until Vapo-Valve clicks, reduce heat to low and cook 8-10 minutes or until fish flakes easily. Remove fish from pan and keep warm. Cook liquid over medium heat until syrupy and pour over steaks.

Serve with rice pilaf, garnished with lemon slices and sprigs of herbs.

• •

1 serving contains:

Cal	Prot	Fat	Carb	Fiber	Chol	Sodium
353	57.5 g	11.7 g	0.7 g	0.03 g	113.5 mg	261 mg

• •

How to Cook

Poaching and pan-cooking are two simple techniques for fish cookery.

Poaching: Cooking in liquid retains the moisture of fish, especially skinless fillets.

How-to: In saucepan or skillet, add enough liquid (water or broth plus wine, if desired) to cover fish. Place over medium high heat and bring to a boil. Gently, add fish. Cover; when Vapo-Valve clicks, remove pan from heat. Do not lift lid. Allow to poach for 10 minutes per inch of thickness at the thickest part.

Pan-cooking: This technique works well for fillets or small, whole fish or steaks.

How-to (A): Place fish and small amount of liquid (wine, broth, sauce or whatever recipe calls for) in skillet. Cover and cook over medium heat until Vapo-Valve clicks, reduce heat to low and cook until fish is done. Allow 10 minutes per inch of thickness at the thickest part, total cooking time.

How-to (B): Preheat skillet over medium heat for 2 to 3 minutes or electric skillet to 375 degrees. Spray pan with non-stick vegetable spray or add a small amount of oil or margarine. Add fish, cover and cook until Vapo-Valve clicks. Reduce heat to low and cook until fish is done, allowing 10 minutes per inch of thickness at the thickest part, total cooking time.

Swordfish Steaks with Basil and Shrimp

Utensil: Small skillet
Yield: 2 servings

4	**medium shrimp**
2	**swordfish steaks**
1	**tablespoon lemon juice**
1	**tablespoon dry vermouth or additional *lemon juice**
6	**fresh basil leaves, minced**
	lemon slices, garnish
	sprigs of basil, garnish

Peel and devein shrimp, cut into quarters, set aside.

Place swordfish steaks in small skillet, mix lemon juice and vermouth, pour over fish. Sprinkle with basil. Scatter shrimp over fish.

Cover; cook over medium heat until Vapo-Valve clicks, reduce heat to low, and cook 12-15 minutes or until fish flakes easily. Place on individual plates; garnish with lemon slices and sprigs of basil.

• •

1 serving contains:

Cal	Prot	Fat	Carb	Fiber	Chol	Sodium
368	60.2 g	11.8 g	1.4 g	0.1 g	137 mg	288 mg

• •

Red Snapper Almondine

Utensil: Electric skillet;
Yield: 4 servings

1/2	**lemon**
4	**red snapper fillets**
1	**cup all-purpose flour**
1	**tablespoon margarine, melted**
1/8	**teaspoon paprika**
1	**tablespoon almond slivers**

Preheat electric skillet to 375 degrees.

Squeeze lemon juice over fish, dip fish in flour; shake off excess flour. Place fish in skillet, drizzle margarine over fish, sprinkle with paprika. Cover; cook until Vapo-Valve clicks, reduce heat to low and cook 8-10 minutes or until fish flakes easily. Gently place fish on serving dish; sprinkle with almonds.

Red Snapper Almondine, Cont.

1 serving contains:

Cal	Prot	Fat	Carb	Fiber	Chol	Sodium
224	20.4 g	5 g	23.1 g	1.2 g	40 mg	96.2 mg

Shrimp Linguine

Utensil: Large skillet
Yield: 8 servings

1	pound medium shrimp
1	(8-ounce) package linguine, uncooked
1/2	cup dry white wine
1	tablespoon lemon juice
1	tablespoon lime juice
1/4	pound fresh snow peas
6	green onions, thinly sliced
1	tablespoon chopped fresh parsley
3/4	teaspoon dried basil leaves
1/2	teaspoon lemon pepper seasoning
2	cloves garlic, minced
1	bay leaf

Peel and devein shrimp.

Prepare linguini according to package directions; drain, set aside.

While linguini is cooking: Combine shrimp, wine, lemon juice and lime juice in skillet. Bring to a boil over medium heat, reduce heat to low, cover and cook 3 minutes. Add remaining ingredients, except linguine. Cook, stirring constantly, just until peas are tender and shrimp are opaque, about 5 minutes. Remove bay leaf from shrimp mixture.

Place hot linguine in a large pasta bowl, top with shrimp.

1 serving contains:

Cal	Prot	Fat	Carb	Fiber	Chol	Sodium
187	17.1 g	1.2 g	23.9 g	1 g	111 mg	179 mg

Parmesan Perch

Utensil: Electric skillet
Yield: 4 servings

1	**pound ocean perch**
2	**tablespoons dry bread crumbs**
1	**tablespoon grated Parmesan cheese**
1	**teaspoon dried basil**
1/2	**teaspoon paprika**
1/8	**teaspoon freshly ground black pepper**
1	**tablespoon olive oil**
2	**tablespoons fresh parsley, chopped**

Preheat electric skillet to 375 degrees. Cut perch into serving size pieces. In a small bowl combine bread crumbs, cheese, basil, paprika and pepper. Brush one side of fish with oil, dip into crumb mixture. Place fish, uncoated side down, in skillet. Cover; cook until Vapo-Valve clicks, reduce heat to low and cook 8-10 minutes or until fish flakes easily. Gently place fish on serving dish, sprinkle with parsley.

1 serving contains:

Cal	Prot	Fat	Carb	Fiber	Chol	Sodium
297	22.4 g	18.6 g	12.2 g	0.5 g	62.5 mg	232 mg

Spanish-Style Catfish

Utensils: Large skillet, Saladmaster Machine
Yield: 2 servings

1/2	**medium green pepper**
1/2	**medium onion**
1	**tablespoon margarine**
1	**whole catfish**
1	**lemon**
1	**clove garlic, minced**
1	**medium tomato, chopped**
1	**teaspoon cilantro, snipped**

Process green pepper and onion using #2 cone.
Melt margarine in skillet over medium heat. Add catfish; brown one side 10 minutes, reduce heat to low. Turn fish; squeeze lemon over fish,

Spanish-Style Catfish, Cont.

top with green pepper, onion, garlic, tomato, and cilantro. Cover; simmer 10-15 minutes or until fish flakes easily.

1 serving contains:

Cal	Prot	Fat	Carb	Fiber	Chol	Sodium
350	42.7 g	15.7 g	9 g	2.1 g	132 mg	227 mg

Oriental Poached Flounder

Utensil: Large skillet
Yield: 4 servings

2	tablespoons reduced-fat or *fat-free French dressing
4	teaspoons reduced- sodium soy sauce
3/4	teaspoon ground ginger
1	pound *flounder or orange roughy fillets

In a small bowl combine French dressing, soy sauce and ginger, stir.
   Arrange fish in cold skillet, pour dressing mixture over fish and marinate 10 minutes. Cover; cook on medium heat until Vapo-Valve clicks, reduce heat to low and cook 8-10 minutes or until fish flakes easily. Pour sauce over fish on serving plate.

1 serving contains:

Cal	Prot	Fat	Carb	Fiber	Chol	Sodium
139	27.8 g	1.8 g	1.5 g	0.02 g	90.7 mg	337 mg

Linguini with Salmon and Garlic

The mild taste of this savory recipe awakens your taste buds.

Utensils: 7-quart Dutch oven, Small skillet
Yield: 4-6 servings

16	ounces canned salmon, or *minced clams
1	tablespoons olive oil
5	cloves garlic, thinly sliced
1/2	cup white wine
1	cup fish broth or clam juice
1/4	cup fresh parsley, minced

8	ounces linguini
2	tablespoons fresh lemon juice
	dash of freshly ground pepper

Drain salmon; reserve liquid (add enough fish broth or chicken broth to make 1/2 cup).

Discard skin from salmon; crush bones and combine with salmon.

Heat small skillet for 2-3 minutes over medium heat, add oil and garlic, sauté; add wine. Reduce heat to low and simmer about 10 minutes

Stir liquid from salmon, broth, and fish into garlic, cook about 10 minutes or until hot. Add parsley, lemon juice, and pepper; cover and remove from heat. Keep warm.

While fish and broth are simmering, cook linguini according to package directions; drain well, place in preheated serving bowl. Toss gently with fish mixture. Serve immediately.

● ●

1 serving contains:

Cal	Prot	Fat	Carb	Fiber	Chol	Sodium
247	16.3 g	3.9 g	32.5 g	1.8 g	27 mg	256 mg

● ●

Tuna Noodle Casserole

Utensils: 3-quart saucepan, Saladmaster Machine
Yield: 4 servings

1	celery stalk
3 1/2	cups noodles
3	tablespoons margarine
1/4	cup fresh mushrooms, minced
2	tablespoons all-purpose flour
1 1/4	cups 2% or *skim milk
1/2	cup frozen peas
1	(6 1/2-ounce) can tuna, packed in water, drained
1/4	cup fresh parsley, minced
1/4	cup crushed cornflakes or *crackers, topping

Process celery using #2 cone.

Prepare noodles according to package directions; drain, set aside.

While noodles are cooking: Melt margarine in pan over medium heat, stir in celery and mushrooms. Cover; when Vapo-Valve clicks, reduce heat to low and cook 5 minutes.

Tuna Noodle Casserole, Cont.

Blend flour with $1/4$ cup cold milk, add to vegetables and cook over medium heat. As mixture thickens, add remaining milk, continue to stir until mixture thickens.

Add peas to sauce and vegetables, cook 2-3 minutes. Stir in tuna and noodles, cook until heated through. Stir in parsley, sprinkle with crushed topping, and serve.

1 serving contains:

Cal	Prot	Fat	Carb	Fiber	Chol	Sodium
462	21.8 g	22.5 g	43.2 g	3.5 g	31.9 mg	705 mg

Festival Shrimp and Saffron Rice

Utensils: Large skillet, Saladmaster Machine
Yield: 2 servings

$1/2$	medium red or *green pepper
$1/2$	pound medium shrimp
1	teaspoon margarine
$1/4$	cup green onion, sliced
1	clove garlic, minced
$1/2$	teaspoon seafood seasoning blend
1 $1/2$	cups cooked rice (cooked with $1/16$ teaspoon ground saffron or *turmeric)
1	tablespoon part-skim Parmesan cheese, grated

Process red pepper using #3 cone.

Peel and devein shrimp.

Melt margarine in skillet over medium heat, add red pepper, onion, and garlic, cook 1 to 2 minutes. Add shrimp and seasoning blend; stir, cook 3 to 4 minutes or until shrimp are opaque. Stir in rice and cheese; cook until thoroughly heated, about 2 to 3 minutes. Garnish as desired.

1 serving contains:

Cal	Prot	Fat	Carb	Fiber	Chol	Sodium
355	29.4 g	3.7 g	48.6 g	1.2 g	224 mg	660 mg

Chicken
Enchiladas

Poultry

Chicken and turkey have long been considered one of the health-conscious eater's best friends. With skin removed, poultry is a relatively low-fat source of protein, especially the white meat.

Moreover, chicken provides a great flavor base for just about every cuisine. Whether you like French, Asian, barbecue, homestyle, Mediterranean or other, more exotic dishes, chicken can often be a calorie-wise beginning of an adventurous meal.

Waterless, no-fat cooking does wonders for chicken as well. Some traditional methods, such as sautéing over high heat, can actually toughen delicate chicken or turkey breasts. Our recipes and techniques are time, money and nutrition-conscious and no food is more adaptable than poultry.

Most of our recipes call for cut-up chicken pieces, often skinless and boneless, and bite-size morsels or ground chicken. Turkey gets its turn, as well, but is often ground.

But our stovetop braising and roasting methods work as well on poultry, as on meats. A whole turkey, Cornish game hens, a roaster or fryer can be prepared on top of the stove. This can come in particularly handy around holidays when stack-cooking makes efficient use of burners for preparing festive family dinners. Using stovetop roasting also frees up the oven for pastries or desserts.

How to cook poultry

There are three basic methods for cooking poultry on top of the stove: braising, range-top roasting and pan-frying (the electric skillet is particularly handy for this).

Braising: This method of first browning then cooking in liquid is particularly good for bone-in pieces or whole birds.

How-to: Preheat pan (usually skillet or Dutch oven) over medium-high heat for 3 to 5 minutes. Cook poultry on all sides until brown. Add 1/4 cup liquid (water, wine, broth, for example) or as required by recipe. Cover; when Vapo-Valve clicks, turn heat to low and cook according to the chart.

Poultry	Minutes per pound
Chicken	
whole, halves, quarter	.20
serving pieces	.20
boneless breasts	.15
Turkey	
whole breast, bone-in pieces	.20
boneless "steaks" or "fillets"	.15
Cornish game hens	
whole, halves	.25
Duck	
whole, halves, pieces	.30

Stovetop roasting: Use this technique for whole birds or bone-pieces that you might otherwise roast in the oven.

How-to: Preheat Dutch oven 3 to 5 minutes over medium heat. Cook poultry on all sides until brown. Meat may stick, but it will loosen as browning continues. Turn gently, using a spatula to loosen skin without tearing. Do not add liquid (unless recipe specifies). Cover; when Vapo-valve clicks, turn heat to low and cook according to the chart.

Poultry	Minutes per pound
Chicken	
whole, halves, quarters	.25

• •

To test for doneness, especially when roasting whole poultry, stuffed or unstuffed, use an instant read meat thermometer. When inserted in meaty part of thigh, thermometer should register 180 to 185 degrees. Center of stuffing should be at least 165 degrees.

Pan-Frying: Saladmaster's unique 7-ply construction allows you to fry chicken without added oil or grease.

How to: Heat electric skillet (large or small skillet) to medium high. To tell when a pan is properly preheated, splash a few drops of water on the surface. If the drops bead and dance, the pan is ready to use. Add chicken pieces, pressing them against bottom and sides of pan. For a healthier option, remove skin and fat before cooking. Meat may stick, but will loosen as browning continues. Place lid on pan slightly ajar. When meat loosens, turn and fry until golden brown about 10 more minutes.

Some safety tips

Cooking with poultry requires some basic knowledge of food safety. Never undercook chicken. Juices should run clear when the meat is pierced with a fork. Carefully wash hands, knives, cutting boards and any utensils that uncooked poultry may come in contact with. This cuts the risk of contaminating another dish with salmonella bacteria, sometimes found on raw poultry.

As with other meats, chicken should be thawed overnight in the refrigerator, when time allows. Be sure and place chicken in a leakproof container so the juices do not touch other foods. For quicker thawing, defrost in the microwave using manufacturer's instructions or thaw under cold, running water.

Crunchy Chicken Fingers

Always in demand, crunchy chicken fingers are a favorite of children and teenagers.

Utensils: Electric skillet, Saladmaster Machine
Yield: 4 servings

$^1/_3$	cup cornflake crumbs
$^1/_2$	cup pecans
1	tablespoon parsley flakes
$^1/_4$	teaspoon garlic powder
2	tablespoons skim milk
4	boneless chicken breasts halves, skinned
1	tablespoon canola oil

Process pecans using #1 cone.

In a shallow bowl, combine cornflake crumbs, pecans, parsley and garlic powder. Pour milk into another shallow bowl; dip chicken strips in milk; coat with crumb mixture.

Heat oil in skillet at 375 degrees. Carefully add breaded chicken to skillet; brown 4-5 minutes. Reduce heat to 275 degrees. Cook until chicken turns loose from skillet; turn.

Cover; cook 5-6 minutes until tender. Remove cover and continue to cook about 5 minutes more until crisp.

• •

1 serving contains:

Cal	Prot	Fat	Carb	Fiber	Chol	Sodium
529	60.5 g	20.8 g	22.8 g	0.9 g	156 mg	372 mg

• •

Crabmeat Chicken Rolls

Utensil: Electric skillet
Yield: 6 servings

1	(6-ounce) can crabmeat
$^1/_4$	cup water chestnuts, finely chopped
2	tablespoons fine dry bread crumbs
2	tablespoons reduced-fat or *fat-free mayonnaise
1	tablespoon fresh parsley, minced
$^1/_4$	teaspoon Dijon mustard
6	boneless chicken breast halves, skinned
$^1/_8$	teaspoon lemon pepper

2 tablespoons white wine or *Worcestershire sauce
3 green onions, chopped
1/8 teaspoon paprika

In a medium bowl combine crabmeat, water chestnuts, bread crumbs, mayonnaise, parsley and mustard; set aside.

Place one piece of chicken between two pieces of waxed paper. Working from the center to the edges, pound lightly with meat mallet to 1/8" thickness. Remove waxed paper and repeat with remaining chicken.

Sprinkle chicken with lemon pepper. Spoon crabmeat filling onto one end of each chicken breast half. Fold in sides; roll up. Arrange chicken in electric skillet, seam side down. Brush with 1 tablespoon Worcestershire sauce. Cover; cook at 350 degrees until Vapo-Valve clicks, reduce heat to 200 degrees and cook 20-25 minutes or until chicken is tender. Brush with remaining Worcestershire sauce; sprinkle with green onions and paprika.

• •
1 serving contains:

Cal	Prot	Fat	Carb	Fiber	Chol	Sodium
373	64 g	8.7 g	6.1 g	.4 g	181 mg	360 mg

• •

Stir-Fry Chicken Dinner with Sweet and Sour Sauce

Utensils: Wok, Saladmaster Machine
Yield: 8 servings

3 celery stalks
1 medium onion
1 medium zucchini
1 large green pepper
6 large mushrooms
1/2 pound fresh snow peas
5 boneless, chicken breast halves, skinned
1 pound fresh broccoli; chopped
2 tablespoons cornstarch
1/2 cup low-fat, low-sodium chicken broth
1 1/4 cups Sweet and Sour Sauce (see recipe below)
8 cups cooked rice

Stir-Fry Chicken Dinner with Sweet and Sour Sauce, Cont.

Process celery using #2 cone, onion, zucchini, pepper and mushrooms using #4 cone.

Remove ends and strings from snow peas.

Cut chicken into 1" wide strips.

Preheat wok on medium-high heat; place chicken in wok. Cover; brown 2 minutes each side. Add broccoli and onion. Cover; cook 3 minutes. Add remaining vegetables; stir well. Cover; cook over medium heat until Vapo-Valve clicks, reduce heat to medium-low and cook 10 minutes.

Remove cover; push chicken/vegetables to sides of wok, making a well in the center of mixture. In a small bowl stir cornstarch and chicken broth to blend, add to skillet, stir. Add Sweet and Sour Sauce to liquid in bottom of wok; stir until slightly thickened. Turn heat off, cover; let stand 2 minutes. Serve over rice.

1 serving contains:

Cal	Prot	Fat	Carb	Fiber	Chol	Sodium
628	46 g	6.1 g	96.7 g	5 g	97.5 mg	185 mg

Sweet and Sour Sauce

Utensil: 1-quart saucepan
Yield: 1 1/4 cups (1 serving: one eighth of recipe)

1/2	cup pineapple juice
1 1/2	tablespoons cornstarch
1/2	cup honey
1	tablespoon reduced-sodium soy sauce
1/4	teaspoon freshly ground black pepper
1/2	cup red wine vinegar
1/4	teaspoon ground ginger
1/4	teaspoon garlic powder
1/4	teaspoon chives

In saucepan mix pineapple juice with cornstarch; add all remaining ingredients. Bring to boil over medium heat; stir continually until thick. Reduce heat to low; simmer 1 minute.

Serve warm or add to stir-fry recipes.

● ●

1 serving contains:

Cal	Prot	Fat	Carb	Fiber	Chol	Sodium
104	0.5 g	0.03 g	27.5 g	0.2 g	0 mg	61.5 mg

● ●

Italian Chicken

Utensil: Large skillet, Saladmaster Machine
Yield: 4 servings

1	**medium green or red pepper**
4	**boneless chicken breast halves, skinned**
1	**(8-ounce) can low-sodium tomato sauce**
1	**tablespoon oregano**
3	**tablespoons cornstarch**
1/3	**cup cold water**
4	**cups cooked rice**

Process green pepper using #3 cone.

Preheat skillet on medium heat, arrange chicken in skillet; press flat. Cook quickly until brown on both sides.

In a small bowl combine pepper, tomato sauce and oregano, pour over chicken. Cover; cook over medium heat until Vapo-Valve clicks, reduce heat to low and cook 40-60 minutes. Uncover; remove chicken.

In a small bowl combine cornstarch and water; stir until smooth. Add to sauce, cook over low heat stirring constantly until thick and bubbly. Serve chicken over rice; top with sauce.

● ●

1 serving contains:

Cal	Prot	Fat	Carb	Fiber	Chol	Sodium
589	60 g	9.02 g	67.7 g	2.1 g	156 mg	144 mg

● ●

Z-z-z-zucchini

To make this a complete meal, slice 3 to 4 zucchini squash and add to pan after chicken is removed. Stir in zucchini, then add cornstarch. Cook until sauce bubbles and thickens. Return chicken to pan and baste with sauce. Serve according to recipe instructions.

Chicken Marsala

Marsala is a fortified Sicilian wine that varies from dry to sweet subtly enhancing the recipe's flavors.

Utensil: Large skillet
Yield: 4 servings

4	boneless chicken breast halves, skinned
1 $1/2$	cups fresh mushrooms, sliced
2	tablespoons green onion, sliced
2	tablespoons water
$1/4$	teaspoon salt
$1/4$	cup Marsala wine or *dry sherry

Place one piece of chicken between two pieces of waxed paper. Working from the center to the edges, pound lightly with meat mallet to about $1/4$" thickness. Remove waxed paper.

Repeat with remaining chicken breast halves.

Preheat skillet over medium heat. Add chicken, cook 5-6 minutes or until chicken is tender. Transfer to platter; keep warm.

Add mushrooms, green onion, water and salt to skillet. Cook over medium heat 3 minutes or until mushrooms are tender and most of liquid has evaporated. Add wine; heat thoroughly. To serve, spoon vegetables and sauce over chicken.

● ●

1 serving contains:

Cal	Prot	Fat	Carb	Fiber	Chol	Sodium
350	58.2 g	8.3 g	3 g	0.5 g	156 mg	272 mg

● ●

Raspberry Chicken

Raspberry, the fruit of gourmets, adds a delicate bouquet and an elegant look to this dish.

Utensils: Large skillet, 1-quart saucepan
Yield: 4 servings

1	cup fresh or *frozen raspberries
1	teaspoon orange peel, finely grated
$1/2$	cup orange juice
$1/2$	teaspoon instant chicken bouillon
$1/8$	teaspoon ground nutmeg

1/8	teaspoon black pepper
4	boneless chicken breast halves, skinned
2	teaspoons cornstarch
1	tablespoon cold water
2 1/2	tablespoons honey

Thaw raspberries if frozen; set aside.

In skillet combine orange peel, orange juice, bouillon, nutmeg and pepper; bring to boil over medium heat; add chicken. Cover; cook until Vapo-Valve clicks, reduce heat to low and cook 25 minutes or until chicken is tender. Turn chicken; cook 10 minutes more.

In saucepan stir together cornstarch, water and honey. Cook over medium heat, stirring constantly until thick and bubbly. Gently stir in raspberries; heat thoroughly. Pour over chicken; serve with rice.

1 serving contains:

Cal	Prot	Fat	Carb	Fiber	Chol	Sodium
395	58.2 g	8.5 g	19.5 g	2.1 g	156 mg	141 mg

Vim and vinegar: To give the Raspberry Chicken a sweet-and-sour twist, stir in 1 or 2 teaspoons raspberry or balsamic vinegar, along with raspberries.

Roast Turkey Breas

Utensils: Medium saucepan, Dutch oven
Yield: 6 to 8 servings

1	(*5- to 7-pound) boneless turkey breast white meat roasted
1	tablespoon *canola oil or margarine
1/2	cup celery, chopped
3/4	cup onion, chopped
1/2	teaspoon poultry seasoning or *sage
2	cups bread cubes, toasted
1	medium apple, cored, unpeeled, chopped

Rinse turkey breast and pat dry. Heat oil or margarine in saucepan over medium heat. Add celery and onion. Cook until celery and onion begin to soften. Add seasoning, bread cubes and apple; toss lightly.

Roast Turkey Breast, Cont.

Stuff cavity under breast with bread cubes. Roll meat and skin around stuffing and secure with toothpicks. Tie with butcher's twine, if desired. Preheat Dutch oven over medium heat for 2 to 3 minutes. Place turkey, breast side down, in pan. Cook until golden, then cover. When Vapo-Valve clicks, reduce heat to low and cook 25 to 30 minutes per pound.

1 serving contains:

Cal	Prot	Fat	Carb	Fiber	Chol	Sodium
506	86 g	11.4 g	9.7 g	1 mg	196	245 mg

Savory Barbecue Chicken and Rice

Utensil: Electric skillet
Yield: 8 servings

8	chicken breast halves, skinned
1	teaspoon seasoning salt
1/2	teaspoon garlic powder
1/2	teaspoon lemon herb seasoning
1 1/2	cups instant rice, uncooked
2	cups barbecue sauce
1	cup water

Preheat electric skillet to 425 degrees. Brown chicken on one side for 15 minutes, turn chicken; add seasonings, cover for 5 minutes. Pour uncooked rice between chicken, pour barbecue sauce over top, add water. Cover, cook until Vapo-Valve clicks, reduce heat to low and cook about 20 minutes, or until chicken and rice are tender.

1 serving contains:

Cal	Prot	Fat	Carb	Fiber	Chol	Sodium
392	55.8 g	7.8 g	21.1 g	0.8 g	146 mg	821 mg

Wine-Poached Chicken

Utensils: 3-quart saucepan, Saladmaster Machine
Yield: 4 servings

3	**medium carrots**
3	**celery stalks**
1 1/2	**small onions**
1	**2 1/2 -*3 pound chicken, cut into serving pieces**
1	**tablespoon fresh tarragon leaves or 1 teaspoon *dried tarragon, minced**
1	**teaspoon dried thyme**
1	**cup dry white wine or *chicken broth**
1-*1 1/2	**cups low-fat, low-sodium chicken broth**
1	**bay leaf**

Process carrots, celery and onions using #2 cone.

Gently mix vegetables; place 1/3 vegetable mixture in saucepan. Layer drumsticks and thighs (separate them at joint, if butcher has not) on top of vegetables. Sprinkle with half of the tarragon. Layer another third of the vegetables, chicken breast and wings, and sprinkle with remaining tarragon. Top with remaining vegetables.

Sprinkle with thyme; pour wine over chicken and add enough chicken broth to just reach breasts and wings. Push bay leaf down into cooking liquid.

Cover; cook over medium heat until Vapo-Valve clicks, reduce heat to low and cook 30 minutes, or until chicken is tender. Serve over rice.

• •

1 serving contains:

Cal	Prot	Fat	Carb	Fiber	Chol	Sodium
717	102 g	25.9 g	12.9 g	3.3 g	304 mg	553 mg

• •

Red or white: Chicken doesn't always require a white wine. For a hearty, winter dish, use dry red wine and chicken broth as the cooking liquid. Substitute parsley for tarragon. Serve with a Beaujolais, a young, fruity French wine.

Chicken with Rice and Peas

Utensils: 7-quart Dutch oven, Saladmaster Machine
Yield: 6 servings

1 1/2	**small onions**
1	**2 1/2-to-*3 pound chicken, cut into serving pieces**
1/2	**teaspoon salt**
	dash of freshly ground black pepper
1	**tablespoon canola oil**
2	**cloves garlic, minced**
2	**teaspoons paprika**
1	**cup tomatoes, finely chopped**
1 1/2	**cups long-grain rice**
1	**cup fresh or frozen peas**
2 1/2	**cups boiling water**
1/8	**teaspoon ground saffron or *turmeric**
2	**tablespoons parsley, finely chopped**

Process onions using #2 cone.

Sprinkle chicken with salt and pepper. Heat Dutch oven over medium heat, and when drops of water dance when sprinkled in pan, add oil. Carefully add chicken, cook quickly until brown on both sides. Remove chicken from pan and set aside.

Add onions and garlic to pan; stir until onions are soft and transparent, but not brown. Stir in paprika, then tomatoes. Bring to a boil, stir frequently; allow most of the liquid to evaporate until mixture thickens.

Add rice, boiling water, and saffron to pan, stir; add chicken. Cover; cook until Vapo-Valve clicks, reduce heat to low and cook 25-35 minutes or until chicken is tender and rice has absorbed liquid. Stir in parsley and peas. Cover and let stand 5-10 minutes before serving directly from pan.

• •

1 serving contains:

Cal	Prot	Fat	Carb	Fiber	Chol	Sodium
727	74.8 g	23.6 g	49 g	2.9 g	212 mg	391 mg

• •

Chicken Cacciatore

Utensils: Large skillet, Saladmaster Machine
Yield: 4 servings

2	small onions
10	medium mushrooms
2	cloves garlic, minced
1	tablespoon olive oil
1	medium green or red pepper, cut into 2-inch strips
2	medium tomatoes, seeded and chopped
1	bay leaf
$1/2$	teaspoon dried basil
$1/4$	teaspoon dried marjoram
$1/8$	teaspoon dried thyme
$1/8$	teaspoon dried oregano
4	chicken breast halves, skinned
1	cup tomato sauce
$1/3$	cup dry white wine or *chicken broth

Process onions using #2 cone, mushrooms using #4 cone.

Heat oil in skillet over medium heat; add onion and garlic; stir often, do not let garlic brown. When onion is limp, add pepper, tomatoes, mushrooms, bay leaf, and herbs.

Lay breasts, meat side down, over vegetables. Pour tomato sauce and wine over all. Cover; cook until Vapo-Valve clicks, reduce heat to low and cook 1 hour or until chicken is tender. Serve over spaghetti, linguine, noodles, or rice.

● ●

1 serving contains:

Cal	Prot	Fat	Carb	Fiber	Chol	Sodium
404	60.3 g	12 g	11.7 g	2.2 g	156 mg	576 mg

● ●

Chicken Enchiladas

Fast becoming a Southwestern must, chicken enchiladas offer a spicy taste without the cholesterol of red meat.

Utensils: Small skillet, large skillet, Saladmaster Machine
Yield: 4 servings

Mild sauce

1 $^3/_4$	cups canned, whole tomatoes with juice
1	small onion, halved
1	hot green or *red chili pepper, seeded
1	tablespoon fresh coriander leaves or *parsley, minced
$^1/_8$	teaspoon ground cumin

Enchiladas

1	medium onion
1	celery stalk
2	radishes
2	boneless chicken breast halves, skinned
2	tablespoons olive oil
1	clove garlic, minced
1	egg or $^1/_4$ cup *egg substitute
1	tablespoon 2% or *skim milk
1	tablespoon fresh coriander leaves, minced
8	corn tortillas
$^1/_4$	cup plain, *reduced-fat or fat-free yogurt
2	tablespoons reduced-fat or *fat-free sour cream
4	green onions, sliced diagonally

Prepare sauce by placing ingredients in a food process or blender and processing until smooth. Pour into small skillet. Cover; cook over medium heat until Vapo-Valve clicks, reduce heat to low and cook 20 minutes. Turn off heat and keep covered.

Process onion and celery using #2 cone, radishes using #4 cone.

While sauce is cooking: Cut chicken into very small pieces. Heat oil in large skillet over medium heat; add onion, celery, and garlic and stir until onion is translucent. Add chicken and stir 5-6 minutes, just until chicken is tender. In a small bowl beat egg with milk and add to pan along with fresh coriander. Stir until egg is nearly set; remove from heat and cover pan.

To assemble enchiladas: Dip corn tortillas, one at a time, in mild sauce only long enough to soften slightly, about 10 seconds. Remove with slotted spatula and place tortilla on work surface; top with portion of chicken filling. Roll up tortilla around filling and place seam side down on serving platter. Repeat with remaining tortillas and chicken filling. Spoon Mild Sauce over enchiladas. Combine yogurt and sour cream and spoon over top, sprinkling with scallions and radish slices as garnish. Serve immediately.

1 serving contains:

Cal	Prot	Fat	Carb	Fiber	Chol	Sodium
443	38.3 g	15.2 g	40.7 g	6.8 g	79.2 mg	301 mg

Spaghetti Sauce with Sweet Red Peppers and Turkey

Utensils: Large skillet, Saladmaster Machine
Yield: 4 servings

1/2	medium onion
1/2	medium red or green pepper
1	tablespoon olive oil
1	cup *turkey breast or dark meat, chopped and cooked
1	cup tomato sauce
1	clove garlic, minced
1/4	teaspoon dried basil
1/4	teaspoon dried oregano
	dash of freshly ground black pepper
	fresh parsley, minced, garnish
	spaghetti

Process onion and pepper using #2 cone.

Heat oil in skillet over medium heat, add onions and red pepper. Sauté, stirring frequently, until onions are lightly browned.

Add turkey, tomato sauce, garlic, basil, oregano, and pepper. Cover; cook until Vapo-Valve clicks, reduce heat to low, and cook 4-5 minutes. Serve over spaghetti and garnish with minced parsley.

1 serving contains:

Cal	Prot	Fat	Carb	Fiber	Chol	Sodium
121	13 g	5.2 g	6.2 g	1.3 g	18.7 mg	755 mg

Turkey Meat Loaf with Tomato Sauce

Utensils: Small skillet, Saladmaster Machine
Yield: 6 servings

1	**small carrot**
1	**medium green pepper**
1	**medium onion**
1	**celery stalk**
1	**pound ground turkey (no skin added)**
1	**clove garlic, minced**
2	**tablespoons fresh parsley, minced**
1	**egg or 2 egg whites or $1/4$ cup *egg substitute, beaten**
$3/4$	**cup brown or *white rice, cooked**
1	**cup +2 tablespoons tomato sauce, divided**
1	**tablespoon reduced-sodium soy sauce**
1	**teaspoon lemon juice**
$1/4$	**teaspoon dried oregano**
$1/8$	**teaspoon dried thyme**
$1/8$	**teaspoon paprika**
$1/8$	**teaspoon ground coriander**

Process carrot using #1 cone, pepper, onion and celery using #2 cone.

In a large mixing bowl, combine all ingredients except 1 cup tomato sauce and pat into even layer in small skillet. Cover; cook over medium heat until Vapo-Valve clicks, reduce heat to low and cook 1 hour. Remove from heat and let stand 10 minutes before serving. Serve tomato sauce on the side.

● ●

1 serving contains:

Cal	Prot	Fat	Carb	Fiber	Chol	Sodium
254	21.6 g	11.8 g	14.8 g	1.8 g	52.3 mg	452 mg

● ●

Turkey Scaloppini with Tomatoes

Utensil: Large skillet
Yield: 2 servings

2	turkey breast fillets, skinned and boned (about ³/4 pound)
	dash of freshly ground pepper
¹/2	cup all-purpose flour
2	teaspoons olive oil
1	cup fresh mushrooms, thinly sliced
1	clove garlic, minced
1	tablespoon fresh parsley, minced
1	tablespoon *fresh basil or ¹/2 teaspoon dried basil, minced
¹/2	cup garden-ripe tomatoes, diced
¹/4	cup dry white or *red wine or chicken broth
2	tablespoons part-skim Parmesan cheese, freshly grated

Place one piece of turkey between two sheets of waxed paper. Working from the center to the edges, pound lightly with a meat mallet to about ¹/4" thickness. Cut fillets in half lengthwise and remove any white tendon; you have two pieces per serving. Dust with a few grindings of fresh pepper, then dredge in flour, shaking to remove excess.

Heat oil in skillet over medium heat; carefully add turkey, cook 2 minutes on each side. Add mushrooms, garlic, parsley, basil, tomatoes, and wine. Cover; cook until Vapo-Valve clicks, reduce heat to low, and cook 30 minutes. Sprinkle fillets with Parmesan cheese and cook an additional 5-10 minutes, until turkey is tender.

• •

1 serving contains:

Cal	Prot	Fat	Carb	Fiber	Chol	Sodium
468	57.2 g	10.6 g	28.9 g	2.2 g	123 mg	162 mg

• •

Pan juices and sauces

As with meats, the juices that accumulate in the pan can make wonderful sauces. See page 6-5 for basic instructions.

"Cream gravy goes" particularly well with "fried chicken." Combine 1 ¹/2 cups skim milk with 3 tablespoons flour, preferably instant dissolving flour, in a container with a tight lid. Shake to combine. When chicken is done, remove from pan and keep warm. Lower heat and stir in milk. Stir and cook until thickened. Season to taste with salt and pepper.

Greek Lemon-Garlic Chicken

Utensil: Large skillet
Yield: 4 servings

4	chicken breasts halves, skinned
1	tablespoon olive oil
1/4	teaspoon salt
	dash of freshly ground pepper
5	cloves garlic, thinly sliced
1	tablespoon fresh parsley, minced
2	lemons, thickly sliced, seeds removed
	parsley sprigs, garnish
	lemon slices, garnish

Heat oil in skillet over medium heat, carefully add chicken breasts, meat side down; cook quickly until brown on both sides.

Sprinkle chicken with salt, pepper, garlic, and parsley and arrange lemon slices over breasts. Cover; cook until Vapo-Valve clicks, reduce heat to low and cook 30 minutes, or until chicken is tender. Garnish with parsley sprigs.

● ●

1 serving contains:

Cal	Prot	Fat	Carb	Fiber	Chol	Sodium
366	58.2 g	11.7 g	4.8 g	0.7 g	156 mg	271 mg

● ●

Strings of gold

Saffron, red threads that lend a beautiful color and subtle flavor to Mediterranean-style dishes, is the world's most expensive spice. By the pound, it is like gold. Even sold a few threads at a time in supermarkets, it can seem like an indulgence. Turmeric will lend the same yellow color for a less expensive price, but with less authenticity.

Mexican Meatballs

Ethnic Dishes

For flavor, economy and nutrition, ethnic dishes offer some of the most enticing recipes. Traditionally, ethnic cuisines have been mostly vegetables and starches, like pasta or rice. Meat is used as a flavoring ingredient instead of a main course. Often, the result is dishes that are lower in fat and meet contemporary nutrition guidelines.

The Food Guide Pyramid (see page XXV) is a visual symbol for healthful eating. At the top are fats and oils, representing foods which should be eaten in very limited amounts. Experts recommend a diet with no more than 30 percent calories from fat, 10 percent being saturated fat.

Saturated fat is found primarily in animal fats and is solid at room temperature. When vegetable fats undergo a process called hydrogenation they can also become saturated fats, although these fats do not contain cholesterol.

Dietary cholesterol is considered by some to be a factor in increasing the amount of cholesterol in the blood. People with high blood cholesterol may be at greater risk for heart disease.

And fats in general are considered to be a problem in the diet because they increase risk for higher blood cholesterol and heart disease, as well as obesity and cancer.

Ethnic and vegetarian dishes (see chapter 4) can be very helpful in meeting these guidelines. This collection represents dishes from the Mediterranean, including Greece, Italy and Spain. South America is represented by dishes from Cuba and Mexico. Asian cuisines reflect Filipino, Oriental and Indian traditions.

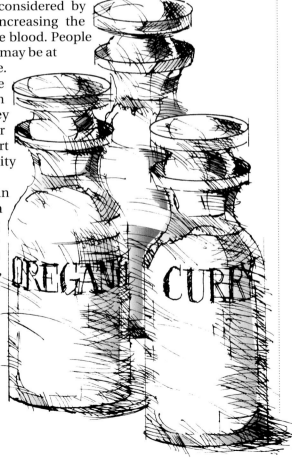

Greek Lamb with Green Beans

Utensils: Electric skillet, Saladmaster Machine
Yield: 8 servings

2	medium onions
2	tablespoons olive oil
3	pounds lean lamb shoulder
1	(6-ounce) can tomato sauce
2	pounds fresh green beans, sliced lengthwise
1/4	cup fresh dill, chopped
1	cup water

Process onions using #2 cone.
   Heat olive oil in skillet at 375 degrees. Cut lamb into 3-inch cubes. Carefully add lamb and onion to skillet; brown lamb on all sides. Reduce heat to 350 degrees, add tomato sauce, green beans, dill and water. Cover; cook until Vapo-Valve clicks, reduce heat to 200 degrees and cook 1 1/2 hours or until meat is tender.

• •
1 serving contains:

Cal	Prot	Fat	Carb	Fiber	Chol	Sodium
566	63.2 g	28.7 g	13.1 g	3.8 g	208 mg	264 mg

• •

German Sauerbraten

Utensils: Electric skillet, Saladmaster Machine
Yield: 8 servings

1	medium onion
1	cup vinegar
1	quart water
3	bay leaves
3	cloves
4	pounds lean round steak
2 1/2	tablespoons canola oil
1/3	cup red wine
1	tablespoon cornstarch

Process onion using #4 cone.

In a small bowl combine onion, vinegar, water, bay leaves and cloves. Place beef in a sealable container; pour marinade over beef. Cover; refrigerate 2-4 days. Turn twice each day.

Remove meat from marinade with a slotted spoon, reserve marinade. Add cornstarch to marinade, stir well.

Heat oil in skillet at 375 degrees. Carefully add meat; cook quickly until brown. Remove meat from skillet; set aside. In skillet add reserved marinade, stir until slightly thick. Add meat. Cover; cook at 325 degrees until Vapo-Valve clicks, reduce heat to 200 degrees and cook 1 - 1 $1/2$ hours. Add wine; cook $1/2$ hour. Strain gravy.

1 serving contains:

Cal	Prot	Fat	Carb	Fiber	Chol	Sodium
679	58.1g	45.7 g	4 g	0.3 g	189 mg	137 mg

Tacoritos

Utensils: Electric skillet, 2-quart saucepan, Small skillet, Saladmaster Machine, Steamer Inset
Yield: 6 servings

4	**ounces reduced-fat or *fat-free cheddar cheese**
1	**medium onion**
$1/2$	**head lettuce**
1	**cup 2% or *skim milk**
$1/8$	**teaspoon white pepper**
1 $1/2$	**teaspoons chili powder**
1	**clove garlic, minced**
2	**tablespoons cream of rice cereal, uncooked**
$1/4$	**teaspoon ground sage**
$1/4$	**teaspoon dried whole oregano**
$1/4$	**teaspoon cumin**
1	**tablespoon green chili pepper, minced**
$1/2$	**pound lean ground beef**
1	**cup tomato, chopped**
6	**6-inch flour tortillas**

Process cheese using #1 cone, onion using #2 cone, lettuce using #4 cone, cover lettuce and refrigerate until ready to use.

Tacoritos, Cont.

In saucepan combine milk, white pepper, chili powder and garlic; bring to a boil over medium heat. Slowly add cereal; cook 1 minute stirring constantly. Pour into container of food processor or blender; process until smooth. Stir in sage, oregano, cumin and chili pepper; set aside.

Cook beef in small skillet over medium heat until brown; stir to crumble meat. Drain meat in steamer inset.

In a large bowl combine meat and onion; add $1/2$ cup cheese and one-half sauce mixture; toss gently. Spoon meat mixture onto each tortilla; roll and place seam side down in electric skillet. Top tortillas evenly with remaining sauce. Cover; bake at 350 for 10 minutes. Uncover; sprinkle tortillas with remaining cheese; bake additional 5 minutes.

Serve with shredded lettuce and chopped tomato.

1 serving contains:

Cal	Prot	Fat	Carb	Fiber	Chol	Sodium
77	20.5 g	10.2 g	27.8 g	2.7 g	36.9 mg	332 mg

Enchilada Bake

Utensils: Electric skillet, Medium gourmet skillet, Saladmaster Machine
Yield: 6 servings

1	ounce reduced-fat or *fat-free mozzarella cheese
1	medium onion
1	medium green pepper
6	mushrooms
1	clove garlic, minced
1	tablespoon margarine
1	(16-ounce) can no-fat pinto beans
1	(14 $1/2$-ounce) can stewed tomatoes
1	tablespoon chili powder
1	teaspoon ground cumin
$1/2$	cup dry white wine
$1/2$	cup reduced-fat or *fat-free cottage cheese
$1/4$	cup reduced-fat or *fat-free sour cream
8	whole wheat corn tortillas or *regular corn tortillas
6	black olives

Process cheese using #1 cone, process onion green pepper and mushrooms using #4 cone.

Melt margarine in medium skillet over medium heat; add onion, garlic, mushrooms and green pepper; sauté until tender. Add beans, tomatoes, spices and wine. Cover; cook until Vapo-Valve clicks, reduce heat to low and cook 30 minutes.

In a medium bowl combine cottage cheese and sour cream.

In electric skillet put layer of tortillas, layer of sauce, 1 1/2 tablespoons of grated cheese and 4 tablespoons of sour cream mixture. Repeat until all tortillas are used, ending with layer of sauce and the remaining sour cream mixture. Top with black olives. Cover; cook at 350 degrees until Vapo-Valve clicks, reduce heat to low and cook 15-20 minutes.

1 serving contains:

Cal	Prot	Fat	Carb	Fiber	Chol	Sodium
286	15.4 g	4.6 g	46.5 g	14 g	1.7 mg	367 mg

Stir-Fried Shrimp

Few things go quicker at a banquet than shrimp. It offers a universal appeal and is a sought-after item throughout the world.

Utensils: Wok, Saladmaster Machine
Yield: 4 servings

3	**cups fresh mushrooms**
1	**pound medium shrimp**
2	**teaspoons canola oil**
2	**cloves garlic, minced**
1	**cup sliced green onions**
1/4	**cup dry white wine**

Process mushrooms using #4 cone.

Shell and devein shrimp.

Place oil in wok; heat over medium-high heat. Add garlic; cook 1 minute, stirring frequently; do not let brown. Add shrimp; stir-fry 1 minute. Add mushrooms, onions and wine; stir-fry 2 minutes or until shrimp are pink and vegetables are crisp/tender. Serve over rice.

1 serving contains:

Cal	Prot	Fat	Carb	Fiber	Chol	Sodium
195	25.6 g	3.8 g	9.8 g	1.5 g	221 mg	261 mg

How to stir-fry

Although the wok is the most traditional utensil for stir-frying, this technique can be accomplished using a skillet. A key to successful stir-frying is to have all ingredients chopped and sauce ingredients measured or mixed before proceeding.

Meats and vegetables should be cut in bite-size pieces of uniform proportions, so they can cook in three to five minutes. Use a broad, flat wooden spoon or spatula to prevent scratching your cookware.

One last tip: limit the oil. Stir-frying has a justifiably healthful reputation as long as the cook doesn't overdo the oil in the pan. Recent criticisms of some dishes in Chinese restaurants has centered on the amount of oil used in the wok for stir-frying. Go easy on the oil and enjoy the taste of fresh vegetables, cooked just until tender, but still crisp.

First, heat a skillet over medium-high heat until drops of water dance when sprinkled in the pan. Then add 2 teaspoons (or desired amount) oil. If using meat or chicken, cook the meat and remove from pan.

Wipe pan clean, heat and add a bit more oil. Begin with vegetables requiring longest cooking times, like carrots, celery or bok choy. Partially cook these before adding more tender, quick-cooking ones, like bean sprouts, Oriental pea pods or spinach.

Stir in sauce, if recipe calls for one, and cook just until thickened. For more tender vegetables, cover skillet and cook on low for a few minutes longer.

Pronto Paella

Utensils: 7-quart Dutch oven, Steamer Inset, Saladmaster Machine
Yield: 6 servings

1	medium onion
1	small red or *green pepper
12	medium shrimp
3/4	pound *Italian sausage, or turkey Italian sausage, sweet or hot, cut into 2-inch pieces
2	cloves garlic, minced
6	chicken drumsticks
2	cups long-grain rice
3	cups chicken broth
	pinch of ground saffron or *turmeric
	dash of freshly ground pepper
2	medium tomatoes, peeled, quartered, and seeded

Process onion and red pepper using #2 cone.

Shell and devein shrimp.

Sauté sausage in Dutch oven over medium heat, browning on all sides until cooked through. Drain off fat using steamer inset. Replace sausage in Dutch oven, add onion, red pepper and garlic; sauté until onion is soft, about 5 minutes. Add chicken and sauté until lightly browned, 6-8 minutes.

Add rice; stir until translucent, about 2 minutes. Stir in broth, saffron, and ground pepper. Cover; cook until Vapo-Valve clicks, reduce heat to low and cook for 20 minutes, until liquid is absorbed.

Fluff paella mixture; add tomatoes and most of the shrimp. Arrange remaining shrimp on top of paella. Cover and continue to cook until shrimp are pink, about 8-10 minutes. Serve with large green salad and whole-grain rolls.

● ●

1 serving contains:

Cal	Prot	Fat	Carb	Fiber	Chol	Sodium
578	37.5 g	21.7 g	55.5 g	2 g	103 mg	991 mg

● ●

Lamb Curry

Curry is a combination of several ground spices such as cayenne pepper, fenugreek, and turmeric. It is often found in dishes from India.

Utensils: Large skillet, Saladmaster Machine
Yield: 4 servings

1	**large onion**
2	**tablespoons canola oil**
3	**cloves garlic, minced**
1	**tablespoon fresh gingerroot or** $1/4$ **teaspoon *ground ginger, minced**
$1/2$	**teaspoon ground coriander**
$1/2$	**teaspoon ground cardamom**
$1/2$	**teaspoon cumin**
$1/4$	**teaspoon ground cinnamon**
$1/4$	**teaspoon chili powder**
$1/4$	**teaspoon turmeric**
$1/2$	**teaspoon salt**
$1/4$	**teaspoon freshly ground black pepper**
1	**pound lamb cubes**
1 $1/2$	**cups chicken broth**
1	**tart green apple, cored**
$1/2$	**cup seedless raisins**

Process onion using #2 cone.

Heat oil in skillet over medium heat; add onion and garlic, sauté until they begin to brown. Add ginger, coriander, cardamom, cumin, cinnamon, chili powder, turmeric, salt, and pepper; stir; add lamb. Turn off heat, cover, and allow meat to marinate for $1/2$ hour.

Process apple using #4 cone.

Add chicken broth and apple to the lamb. Cover; cook over medium heat until Vapo-Valve clicks, reduce heat to low and cook 1 hour. Stir in raisins, cook 30 minutes more. Serve over brown rice with a green salad.

● ●

1 serving contains:

Cal	Prot	Fat	Carb	Fiber	Chol	Sodium
599	27.3 g	42.4 g	26.9 g	3 g	103 mg	644 mg

● ●

Pork and Cashew Stir-Fry

Utensils: Large skillet, Saladmaster Machine
Yield: 4 servings

1	medium onion
3	medium carrots
1	pound boneless pork loin, cut in very thin strips
2	tablespoons dry sherry or *orange juice
1	tablespoon cornstarch
1	tablespoon reduced-sodium soy sauce
1	clove garlic, minced
2	tablespoons peanut or *canola oil
2/3	cup chicken broth
1	tablespoon packed dark brown sugar
1	large green pepper, cut into thin, 2-inch strips
1/2	cup unsalted cashews

Process onion and carrots using #4 cone.

In a small bowl combine sherry, cornstarch, soy sauce, and garlic; pour over pork. Cover and refrigerate 1 hour.

Heat oil in large skillet over medium heat. Add onion; sauté until onions begin to soften. Stir in marinated pork mixture and stir-fry until meat is lightly browned. Add carrots, broth, and brown sugar; stir well. Cover; cook until Vapo-Valve clicks, reduce heat to low, and cook 6-8 minutes or until pork is cooked through. Return heat to medium. Add green pepper; stir 1-2 minutes until crisp-tender. Stir in cashews before serving. Serve over brown rice.

• •
1 serving contains:

Cal	Prot	Fat	Carb	Fiber	Chol	Sodium
652	31.2 g	49.8 g	20.1 g	3.4 g	117 mg	353 mg

• •

Szechwan Pork and Peanut Stir-Fry: Add 1/4 teaspoon or more dried crushed red pepper flakes with carrots and broth. Substitute unsalted peanuts for cashews.

Spicy Tofu
in Indonesian Peanut Sauce

Utensil: 3-quart saucepan
Yield: 6 servings

1	tablespoon olive oil
2	tablespoons fresh gingerroot, minced
3	cloves garlic, minced
2	hot green chili peppers, seeded and minced
1	cup green onions, thinly sliced
2	cups water
1	cup red or *green pepper, thinly sliced cut in 2-inch lengths
2/3	cup chunky natural peanut butter
1	tablespoon lemon juice
1	tablespoon reduced-sodium soy sauce
1	tablespoon packed brown sugar
1	pound tofu, cubed
1/4-1/2	teaspoon crushed dried red pepper flakes (optional)

Heat saucepan over medium heat until drops of water dance when sprinkled in pan. Add oil, and when hot, add minced ginger, garlic, and chili peppers to pan and stir until lightly browned, about 2 minutes. Add green onions; stir another 1-2 minutes.

Add water, stir, add red peppers, peanut butter, lemon juice, soy sauce, and brown sugar. Stir over medium heat until sauce thickens and begins to simmer. Stir in cubed tofu. Cover; reduce heat to low and cook 10 minutes, or just until peppers are tender. Stir and check for flavor. If a spicier dish is desired, add crushed hot chili peppers. Serve over rice.

NOTE: Spicy Tofu is even more flavorful when refrigerated overnight and reheated.

• •

1 serving contains:

Cal	Prot	Fat	Carb	Fiber	Chol	Sodium
287	14.3 g	20.2 g	17.5 g	3.7 g	0 mg	226 mg

• •

Vegetable Curry with Yogurt Sauce

Utensils: 3-quart saucepan, Saladmaster Machine
Yield: 4 servings

1	large onion
2	medium carrots
1	tablespoon margarine
2	cloves garlic, minced
2	teaspoons curry
1/2	teaspoon ground cinnamon
2	cups low-fat, low-sodium chicken broth
1/2	cup long-grain rice
1	tomato, cored and chopped
1	cup cooked and drained chick peas
1/2	cup raisins
1 1/2	cups tiny cauliflower florets
1	cup *fresh or frozen green peas
1	cup plain *reduced-fat or fat-free yogurt
1/2	cup cucumber, grated
1/8	teaspoon black pepper
2	teaspoons lemon juice
2	tablespoons parsley, minced

Process onion using #2 cone, carrots using #4 cone.

Melt margarine in saucepan over medium heat; add onion, sauté until soft. Add garlic, curry powder, and cinnamon, cook 2 minutes more, stirring often.

Add chicken broth, rice, tomato, and carrots; bring to a simmer. Add chick peas and raisins. Cover; cook until Vapo-Valve clicks, reduce heat to low and cook for 15 minutes. Add cauliflower and peas, cover again, and cook 10 minutes longer.

In a small bowl combine the yogurt, cucumber, and pepper; set aside.

Stir lemon juice into the curry and spoon the curry onto a serving platter. Garnish with parsley. Serve the sauce in a separate bowl.

● ●

1 serving contains:

Cal	Prot	Fat	Carb	Fiber	Chol	Sodium
369	14.5 g	5.7 g	68.3 g	10 g	3.9 mg	137 mg

● ●

Vegetable Chow Mein

Utensils: Large skillet, Saladmaster Machine
Yield: 4 servings

2	celery stalks
2	small carrots
1/4	pound mushrooms
4	ounces Oriental egg noodles or *thin egg noodles
1	tablespoon peanut or *canola oil
3	green onions, whites chopped fine, with tops sliced and reserved
2	cloves garlic, minced
1	teaspoon fresh ginger or 1/4 teaspoon *ground ginger, minced
1	cup low-fat, low-sodium chicken broth or *water
2	cups broccoli florets
1	tablespoon cornstarch
1	tablespoon low-sodium soy sauce
1	tablespoon dry sherry
1	teaspoon Oriental sesame or *peanut oil
1/2	teaspoon sugar
1/2	pound firm tofu, cut into 3/4- inch cubes

Process celery, carrots and mushrooms using #4 cone.

Cook noodles, omitting the salt; drain and set aside. While the noodles are cooking: Heat peanut oil in skillet over medium-high heat for 1 minute. Carefully add whites of green onions (reserve green tops), garlic, and ginger. Cook, stirring, for 30 seconds. Add celery, carrots, and mushrooms; stir-fry 2 minutes longer. Stir in 1/2 cup chicken broth, cover, and simmer for 3 minutes. Add broccoli, cover, and simmer for 2 minutes.

In a small bowl, combine remaining chicken broth, cornstarch, soy sauce, sherry, sesame oil, and sugar; add to vegetables. Cook, stirring constantly, over medium heat until thick–about 4 minutes. Add cooked noodles and tofu; cover; simmer for 2 minutes or until the tofu is heated through. Spoon onto serving platter; sprinkle with the reserved green onion tops.

● ●

1 serving contains:

Cal	Prot	Fat	Carb	Fiber	Chol	Sodium
182	8.9 g	8.1 g	20.4 g	5 g	8.9 mg	170 mg

● ●

Chicken Adobo

Saladmaster cookware is enjoyed by cooks around the world. This recipe is a favorite among Filipinos.

Utensils: 4-quart Roaster, Saladmaster Machine
Yield: 4 servings

1/2	**medium onion**
1	**(2 1/2-*3 pounds) chicken, cut into serving pieces**
	ground black pepper to taste
7	**cloves garlic, minced**
1/2	**cup apple cider vinegar**
1/3	**cup reduced-sodium soy sauce**
	vegetable spray
7	**cloves garlic, minced**
1	**teaspoon oregano**
	vegetable spray

Process onion using #2 cone

Rub pepper into chicken and place in 4-quart roaster. In a small bowl mix soy sauce and vinegar; pour over chicken. Cover; cook over medium heat until Vapo-Valve clicks, reduce heat to low and cook for 20 minutes. Remove from heat; place chicken and gravy in a separate container. Return roaster to medium heat; spray cooking spray on the bottom of roaster when it is dry and hot. Add garlic and onion; sauté until onion is tender. Return chicken and gravy to roaster. Cover add oregano, cook for another 15 minutes.

• •
1 serving contains:

Cal	Prot	Fat	Carb	Fiber	Chol	Sodium
685	101 g	25.4 g	8.3 g	0.4 g	304 mg	926 mg

• •

Korean Chicken

Utensil: Large skillet
Yield: 4 servings

1/4	cup green onions, minced
2	tablespoons reduced-sodium soy sauce
1	tablespoon honey
7	cloves garlic, minced
1	tablespoon fresh ginger or 1/2 teaspoon *ground ginger, minced
1/4	teaspoon freshly ground black pepper
2	teaspoons dark *sesame oil (or 2 teaspoons canola oil plus 1 teaspoon sesame seeds)
1	small carrot, cut in julienne strips
4	boneless chicken breast halves, skinned

Combine green onions, soy sauce, honey, garlic, ginger, and pepper. In large skillet, heat sesame oil. If using oil and sesame seeds, heat until seeds begin to brown. Add carrot and stir 1-2 minutes over medium heat, then add green onion mixture. Place chicken breasts in pan; turn breasts once to coat well with marinade before cooking.

Cover; cook over medium heat until Vapo-Valve clicks. Reduce heat to low and cook about 20 minutes or until chicken is tender. Serve, with sauce, over rice.

● ●

1 serving contains:

Cal	Prot	Fat	Carb	Fiber	Chol	Sodium
349	54.7 g	8.6 g	10.4 g	0.9 g	146 mg	374 mg

● ●

Pancit Canton (Flour Stick Noodles)

Utensils: Wok, Saladmaster Machine
Yield: 6 servings

$1/2$	**onion**
1	**celery stalk**
2	**medium carrots**
$1/4$	**red or *green peppers**
$1/4$	**head of cabbage**
	vegetable spray
7	**cloves garlic, minced**
1	**tablespoon gingerroot, thinly sliced**
$1/4$	**cup broccoli florets**
$1/4$	**cup cauliflower**
$1/4$	**cup sweet peas**
$1/4$	**cup reduced- sodium soy sauce**
2	**tablespoons oyster sauce**
	freshly ground black pepper
1	**cup low-fat, low-sodium chicken broth**
2	**chicken breast halves, cooked, boned**
$1/4$	**pound steamed shrimp, shelled and deveined**
1	**(8-ounce) package flour stick noodles**
$1/4$	**cup fresh lemon juice**
	vegetable spray

Process onion and celery using #2 cone, carrots and red pepper using #4 cone, cabbage using #5 cone.

Place wok on medium-high heat, spray with cooking spray. Add garlic, onion and ginger, sauté until tender but not brown. Add all the remaining vegetables, season with soy sauce, Oyster sauce, black pepper and $1/2$ cup of chicken broth. Cover and cook about 5 minutes, stirring periodically.

Slice chicken lengthwise about $1/4$" thick. Add chicken and shrimp to wok. Cover; cook about 2 minutes. Add noodles and the remaining chicken broth, mix well. Cook uncovered until the noodles are tender. Stir in lemon juice before serving.

● ●

1 serving contains:

Cal	Prot	Fat	Carb	Fiber	Chol	Sodium
379	29.6 g	14.7 g	32.8 g	4.3 g	89 mg	947 mg

● ●

Mexican Meatballs

Utensil: Large skillet, Saladmaster Machine
Yield: 8 servings

2	**small hot chili peppers, seeded**
1	**sweet red pepper**
1	**small onion**
1	**pound lean beef or turkey, ground**
$1/2$	**cup yellow cornmeal**
1	**egg or $1/4$ cup egg substitute, slightly beaten**
2	**tablespoons fresh parsley, minced**
1	**tablespoon tomato paste**
$1/4$	**teaspoon ground cumin**
$1/8$	**teaspoon freshly ground black pepper**
4	**tomatoes, chopped**
3	**cloves garlic, minced**
2	**cups tomato sauce**
$1 1/2$	**cups corn**
2	**tablespoons fresh coriander, minced (optional)**
$1/4$	**teaspoon dried hot red pepper flakes, crushed**

Process chili peppers using #1 cone, red pepper and onion #2 cone.

In medium bowl, combine beef, cornmeal, egg, parsley, tomato paste, cumin, and black pepper, set aside.

Place chili peppers, red pepper, onion, tomatoes, and garlic in large skillet. Cover; cook over medium heat until Vapo-Valve clicks, reduce heat to low and cook 10 minutes. Stir in tomato sauce.

Form beef mixture into 16 meatballs, place in tomato-vegetable sauce in skillet. Cover; cook over medium heat, until Vapo-Valve clicks, reduce heat to low and cook for 25 minutes. Add corn, cook 5 minutes more. Stir in fresh coriander, red pepper flakes. Serve over rice or polenta accompany with a green salad.

● ●

1 serving contains:

Cal	Prot	Fat	Carb	Fiber	Chol	Sodium
246	17.9 g	11.6 g	19.3 g	3.3 g	49.5 mg	477 mg

● ●

Poached Pear

Desserts

L ife is short. Eat dessert first." That is the rallying cry of dessert lovers. Satisfying a natural sweet tooth without consuming too much sugar or fat is a challenge. For that reason, relying on the natural sweetness of fruits makes a lot of sense.

Of course, not all fruit desserts are simply fruit. Consider such flavorful recipes as Blushing Poached Peaches, Blueberry Compote with Dumplings and Raspberry Yogurt Parfait. These delicious, fruity desserts can also count toward the recommended five-a-day servings of fruits and vegetables, something authorities consider desirable for a healthy diet. Plus, you get the nutritional bonus of fiber.

For creamy taste with low-fat nutrition, consider our recipes for Chocolate Mint Parfait, Tapioca Custard and Rice Pudding. You'll be surprised that low-fat milk can taste so rich and satisfying.

Cake lovers will find an inviting Pineapple Upside-Down Cake, made simply with the electric skillet, and a Pumpkin Cake with a deceptively easy and nutritious icing.

It is hard to stick to a low-fat eating plan when you deprive yourself of sweet treats. These delicious recipes allow you to indulge without guilt.

Puerto Rican Flan

This caramel-type custard is a staple of Saladmaster dinners in Puerto Rico.

Utensils: Electric skillet, 11-inch utility rack, Pudding pan
Yield: 6-8 servings

1	cup sugar
4	cups + 2 tablespoons water
3	eggs
1	(14-ounce) can condensed milk
1	(12-ounce) can evaporated milk
1/4	teaspoon salt
1/2	teaspoon vanilla
4	cups water

In pudding pan blend sugar and 2 tablespoons of water. Heat on medium, stirring until sugar becomes brown and melts into caramel.

In a medium bowl combine eggs and condensed milk. Add evaporated milk, salt and vanilla; blend. Pour mixture over caramel in pudding pan.

Pour water into skillet; insert utility rack. Heat to boil at 225 degrees. Place pudding pan on utility rack; steam 15 minutes or until toothpick inserted in center comes out clean. Do not overcook.

● ●

1 serving contains:

Cal	Prot	Fat	Carb	Fiber	Chol	Sodium
343	9.2 g	9.4 g	56.6 g	0 g	109 mg	199 mg

● ●

Fruit Compote

Utensils: 3-quart saucepan, Saladmaster Machine
Yield: 6 servings

1	large orange
1/2	cup sugar
1	cup water
2	3- inch cinnamon sticks
3	large tart green apples, cored
1	cup pitted prunes, halved
1/2	cup dried apricots, halved

Using #1 cone, process orange to make 1 tablespoon grated peel; be careful not to cut into white part of peel. Squeeze orange to get 1 cup orange juice. Process apples using #4 cone.

In saucepan combine orange peel and juice, sugar, orange juice, water, and cinnamon sticks. Cook over medium heat, stirring until sugar dissolves. Continue to cook, uncovered, 5 minutes. Add apple slices, prunes and apricots. Cover; cook until Vapo-Valve clicks, reduce heat to low and cook about 20 minutes. Serve warm.

1 serving contains:

Cal	Prot	Fat	Carb	Fiber	Chol	Sodium
235	1.8 g	0.6 g	61.4 g	7.1 g	0 mg	3.9 mg

Raspberry Yogurt Parfaits

Utensil: 2-quart saucepan
Yield: 8 servings

3/4	cup water
3/4	*cup instant rice
16	ounces *reduced-fat or fat-free raspberry yogurt
2	cups fresh raspberries

Place water in saucepan; bring to a boil; stir in rice. Cover; remove from heat and set aside for 5 minutes or until all liquid is absorbed. Cool to room temperature.

Stir yogurt into rice; refrigerate at least 30 minutes. Just before serving, layer rice mixture and berries in parfait glasses or dessert dishes.

*Or use 1 1/2 cups cooked long-grain rice.

1 serving contains:

Cal	Prot	Fat	Carb	Fiber	Chol	Sodium
136	4 g	0.9 g	28.2 g	2.2 g	2.5 mg	32.1 mg

Blushing Poached Peaches

Utensils: 2-quart saucepan, Saladmaster Machine
Yield: 4 servings

1	**large orange**
4	**firm peaches**
2	**tablespoons dry red wine or additional *orange juice**
2	**tablespoons honey**
2	**tablespoons maple syrup**
1	**teaspoon cinnamon**
4	**mint sprigs, garnish**

Process a small section of the orange using #1 cone to make $1/2$ teaspoon grated orange peel. Using a vegetable peeler, cut 4 thin strips from orange peel to be used for garnish; squeeze orange to get $3/4$ cup juice. Set aside.

Cut around top of each peach, about $1/3$ the way down, twist top slightly to free pit, remove pit and discard. Set tops aside. Remove very thin slice from bottom of each peach, stand upright in saucepan.

Stir together orange juice, wine, orange peel, honey, maple syrup, and cinnamon until thoroughly combined. Pour half of sauce over peach halves, replace peach tops, pour remaining sauce over peaches. Cover; cook over medium heat until Vapo-Valve clicks, reduce heat to low, and cook 20-25 minutes or until peaches are quite tender. With slotted spoon, carefully remove peaches from pan and place in individual dessert dishes. Increase heat to medium; cook sauce, uncovered until reduced by half, stirring frequently. Spoon over each peach.

Cool; refrigerate at least 1-2 hours before serving. Garnish with strips of orange rind and mint sprigs at stem end of peaches.

● ●

1 serving contains:

Cal	Prot	Fat	Carb	Fiber	Chol	Sodium
116	1 g	0.1 g	29.3 g	2.4 g	0 mg	2.1 mg

● ●

Tapioca Custard

Utensil: 1-quart saucepan
Yield: 4 servings

3	tablespoons quick-cooking tapioca
1/3	cup sugar
2	eggs, beaten or 1/2 cup egg substitute
2	cups 2% or skim milk
1/2	teaspoon vanilla extract

Combine tapioca, sugar, eggs, and milk in saucepan. Cook over medium heat for 7 minutes, stirring once or twice. Cook 5 minutes longer, stirring frequently.

Remove from heat and stir in vanilla extract. Tapioca thickens as it cools, but it can be served warm. Serve plain or with topping of choice.

1 serving contains:

Cal	Prot	Fat	Carb	Fiber	Chol	Sodium
170	7.3 g	2.7 g	29 g	0.08 g	108 mg	94 mg

Applesauce

Utensils: 1-quart saucepan, Saladmaster Machine
Yield: 4 servings

4	apples, cored
1/4	teaspoon ground cinnamon

Process apples using #2 cone, skin side toward cone.

Place apple and cinnamon in saucepan. Cover; cook on medium heat until Vapo-Valve clicks, reduce heat to low and cook 15-20 minutes.

1 serving contains:

Cal	Prot	Fat	Carb	Fiber	Chol	Sodium
80.4	0.3 g	0.5 g	21.1 g	3.5 g	0 mg	1 mg

Blueberry Compote with Dumplings

This compote with dumplings makes a terrific high-tea dessert.

Utensils: Large skillet, Saladmaster Machine
Yield: 8 servings

1	lemon
1/4	cup whole wheat flour
3/4	cup all-purpose flour
1 1/2	teaspoons baking powder
1/3	cup + 2 tablespoons sugar
1/3	cup 2% or skim milk
1	egg or 1/4 cup *egg substitute
1/3	cup margarine, divided
1	teaspoon cinnamon
2	cups boiling water
2	cups *fresh or frozen blueberries

Process lemon using #1 cone to make 1/4 teaspoon grated lemon peel. Squeeze lemon to make 3 tablespoons juice; set aside.

In a medium bowl combine both kinds of flour, baking powder and 2 tablespoons sugar; set aside. In a small bowl combine milk and egg; set aside.

Melt 2 tablespoons margarine in skillet over low heat; in a small bowl combine remaining sugar, cornstarch, and cinnamon, quickly stir into margarine. Slowly add water, stirring constantly. Increase heat to medium, cook until mixture begins to bubble and becomes translucent. Add lemon juice, lemon peel, and blueberries. Cover; cook until Vapo-Valve clicks.

While blueberries are cooking combine remaining softened margarine with flour until mixture is crumbly. Add milk and egg; stir lightly, just until flour is well moistened. When Vapo-Valve clicks, remove cover and drop batter by tablespoons into blueberries, forming 8 large dumplings.

Cover; reduce heat to low, and cook 20 minutes. To serve, spoon dumplings into serving bowls and top with blueberry compote. Serve warm.

1 serving contains:

Cal	Prot	Fat	Carb	Fiber	Chol	Sodium
200	3.2 g	8.5 g	29.1 g	2 g	26.8 mg	179 mg

Steamed Health Pudding

Utensils: Saladmaster Machine, Pudding pan, 3-quart saucepan
Yield: 6-8 servings

1	**large potato**
1	**large carrot**
1	**large apple, cored**
	vegetable spray
1	**cup chopped dates**
1	**cup raisins**
1/2	**cup margarine, melted**
1 1/4	**cups sugar**
2 1/2	**cups all-purpose flour**
1/4	**teaspoon salt**
2	**teaspoons baking soda**
5	**teaspoons pumpkin pie spice**
4	**cups water**
	nuts or cranberries (optional)

Process potatoes, carrots and apples using #1 cone.
Spray pudding pan with vegetable spray.
In a medium bowl combine potatoes, carrots, apples, dates and raisins; mix well. Stir in margarine and sugar. In a small bowl combine flour, salt, baking soda and spice, Add to vegetable/fruit mixture; stir well. Pour batter into pudding pan.
Pour water into saucepan; bring to boil over medium heat. Insert pudding pan over boiling water, cover; steam 80 minutes. Top with nuts or cranberries, if desired.

• •
1 serving contains:

Cal	Prot	Fat	Carb	Fiber	Chol	Sodium
513	5.5 g	12.2 g	100 g	5.2 g	0 mg	435 mg

• •

Low-fat topping

Plain reduced or fat-free yogurt can make a delicious topping. Stir brown sugar and vanilla into yogurt. For an 8-ounce carton, add 2 to 3 tablespoons sugar and 1 to 2 teaspoons vanilla or to taste. Spoon over pudding. For a firmer topping, drain flavored yogurt as for Yogurt Cream.

Pumpkin Cake

Don't relegate pumpkin cake to just a seasonal status. It is great throughout the year using either fresh or canned pumpkin.

Utensil: Electric skillet
Yield: 10-12 servings

Cake
1	box white cake mix
5	egg whites
1	cup canned pumpkin
1/2	cup fat-free sour cream
1/3	cup orange juice
1	teaspoon cinnamon
1/4	teaspoon cloves
1/2	teaspoon ginger
1/2	teaspoon allspice
1/4	teaspoon nutmeg
2	teaspoons vanilla
	vegetable spray

Icing
2	tablespoons reduced-fat margarine
1	cup powdered sugar
1/4	teaspoon vanilla

Preheat electric skillet to 225 degrees.

In a large bowl combine all cake ingredients (except vegetable spray). Using electric mixer, blend on medium speed for 30 seconds to moisten ingredients. Beat on high speed for 3 minutes.

Spray skillet with cooking spray. Pour in cake batter, spread evenly in skillet. Cover, bake for 1 hour or until wooden pick comes out clean. Shake skillet to loosen cake, immediately turn upside down onto cake plate. Cool.

Combine all icing ingredients in a small bowl, beat until smooth. Gently spread icing over cooled cake.

● ●

1 serving contains:

Cal	Prot	Fat	Carb	Fiber	Chol	Sodium
199	4.3 g	7 g	30.4 g	0.5 g	0 mg	230 mg

● ●

NOTE: Let cake cool completely before icing.

Pineapple Upside-Down Cake

Another Saladmaster dinner party "institution" for many years.

Utensil: Electric skillet
Yield: 10-12 servings

4	tablespoons margarine
1	cup brown sugar
1	(16-ounce) can sliced pineapple, drain and reserve juice
8	maraschino cherries
2	egg whites
1	box *white or yellow cake mix

Melt margarine in skillet at 200 degrees; add sugar; stir. Spread mixture evenly over bottom of skillet. Place 8 pineapple slices symmetrically in skillet. Place maraschino cherries in middle of each ring.

In a medium bowl combine egg whites and cake mix. Prepare according to package directions, using reserved pineapple juice for liquid called for.

Increase electric skillet heat to 350 degrees. Pour batter into skillet over pineapple; cover and cook 6-8 minutes. Reduce heat to 250 degrees; continue to cook 6-8 minutes or until cake is done when tested with a wooden pick. Shake skillet gently to loosen cake; immediately turn upside down onto cake plate, and remove skillet.

• •

1 serving contains:

Cal	Prot	Fat	Carb	Fiber	Chol	Sodium
267	2.3 g	9.8 g	44.2 g	0.5 g	0 mg	247 mg

• •

Add some fruit

This creamy dessert can be further enhanced by a simple garnish of berries. Use beautiful, big, fresh strawberries, luscious raspberries or blackberries in season or dark, plump blueberries.

Apple Oatmeal Bake

Utensils: Electric skillet, Saladmaster Machine
Yield: 6 servings

1/3	cup pecans
3	large apples, cored, sliced 1/4" thick
2	tablespoons fresh lemon juice
1/4	teaspoon ground cinnamon
2/3	cup all-purpose flour
1/3	cup margarine
1/4	cup honey
1/4	cup brown sugar, firmly packed
1/2	cup old- fashioned oatmeal, uncooked

Process pecans using #1 cone, set aside.

Preheat electric skillet at 375 degrees. Place apple slices in skillet. Sprinkle with lemon juice and cinnamon.

In a large bowl blend flour and margarine with a pastry blender until crumbly; add honey, brown sugar and oatmeal. Spread over fruit; cover. Reduce heat to 250 degrees and bake 30 minutes or until apples are tender. Top with pecans.

● ●

1 serving contains:

Cal	Prot	Fat	Carb	Fiber	Chol	Sodium
309	2.6 g	15.1 g	44.4 g	2.9 g	0 mg	172 mg

● ●

Rice Pudding

Utensils: 1-quart saucepan, 3-quart saucepan
Yield: 6 servings

3	cups 2% or*skim milk
1	large stick cinnamon
1	cup long-grain rice, uncooked
2	cups water
1/8	teaspoon salt
	peel of an orange or lemon
3/4	cup sugar
1/4	cup raisins
2	tablespoons dark rum

Heat milk and cinnamon in 1-quart saucepan over low heat until milk is infused with flavor of cinnamon, about 15 minutes.(Do not let milk boil). Strain, set aside.

Combine rice, water, and salt in 3-quart saucepan, bring to a boil over medium heat, stirring occasionally. Place orange peel on top of rice, reduce heat to low; cover and simmer 15 minutes or until rice is tender and liquid is absorbed. Remove and discard orange peel. Add milk and sugar, cover. Cook over medium heat until Vapo-Valve clicks, reduce heat to low and simmer 20 minutes or until thickened, stirring often. Add raisins and rum; cover and simmer 10 minutes more.

Serve hot. Garnish as desired. To reheat, add a little milk to restore creamy texture.

1 serving contains:

Cal	Prot	Fat	Carb	Fiber	Chol	Sodium
284	6.6 g	0.5 g	61.4 g	0.9 g	2 mg	111 mg

Poached Dried Fruit Compote

Utensil: 2-quart saucepan
Yield: 6 servings

8	ounces mixed dried fruit, such as apricots, pears, apples and prunes
1 1/2	cups water
1/2	cup white Riesling or *Rhine wine**
2	cinnamon sticks
4	whole cloves

Combine all ingredients in saucepan. Cover; cook over medium heat until Vapo-Valve clicks. Reduce heat to low, uncover and cook 12 to 15 minutes or until fruit is tender. Cool. Discard cinnamon sticks and cloves.

Serve warm, at room temperature or chilled in individual dessert bowls. Garnish with additional cinnamon sticks, if desired.

1 serving contains:

Cal	Prot	Fat	Carb	Fiber	Chol	Sodium
113	1.2 g	0.2 g	26.4 g	1.4 g	0 mg	8.7 mg

** You may substitute white grape juice for wine.

Chocolate Mint Parfaits

Utensil: 2-quart saucepan
Yield: 7 servings

2/3	**cup sugar**
1/4	**cup cocoa**
3	**tablespoons cornstarch**
	dash salt
2 1/2	**cups 2% or *skim milk, divided**
1	**tablespoon margarine**
1 1/2	**teaspoons vanilla extract, divided**
1	**(1.3-ounce) envelope whipped topping mix**
1/4	**teaspoon mint extract**
3 - 4	**drops red food color**

Combine sugar, cocoa, cornstarch and salt in saucepan; gradually stir in 2 cups of milk. Cook over medium heat, stirring constantly until mixture thickens and boils; boil 1 minute. Remove from heat; stir in margarine and 1 teaspoon vanilla. Pour into medium bowl; lay a piece of wax paper over pudding to prevent a film from forming. Refrigerate until cooled.

In small bowl, combine topping mix, remaining 1/2 cup cold skim milk and remaining 1/2 teaspoon vanilla; prepare according to package directions. Fold 1/2 cup whipped topping into cooled pudding. Blend mint extract and red food color into remaining topping. Alternately spoon chocolate pudding and mint whipped topping into parfait glasses. Refrigerate.

● ●

1 serving contains:

Cal	Prot	Fat	Carb	Fiber	Chol	Sodium
147	3.8 g	2.9 g	27.8 g	0.9 g	2.5 mg	72.4 mg

● ●

Other Saladmaster Products
Accessories

Pizza Pan: Durable stainless steel won't chip or rust. Gleaming finish cleans easily and stays bright.

Electric Skillet High Dome Cover: Provides greater flexibility and space for large quantity cooking in your Saladmaster Electric Skillet.

Bake & Roast Pan: Multi-purpose pan for roasting, broiling and baking items such as large cakes, corn bread, rolls and casseroles.

Oval Baking Dish: This stainless steel baking dish is beautiful and durable. For your at-home entertaining, it will have dozens of uses.

The Gourmet Trio: A true delight for the culinary artist. Eight-inch, 10-inch, and 12-inch skillets are best for sautéing or preparing crepes. Covers are available for all skillets.

Mixing Bowl Set: 1-, 2- and 3-quart stainless steel bowls are designed for use with electric mixers or wonderful for hand stirring. Ring handles provide for convenient storage. A large 5-quart stainless steel mixing bowl is also available, individually.

Bakeware Set: Set includes two 9-inch cake pans, two 9-inch pie pans with large juice-saver rims and one cookie sheet 12 $1/2$-inch X 14 $1/2$-inch.

Jet Coffeemaker: Automatic coffee system features modern engineered design...an exclusive "jet pump" for rich coffee without boiling.

Kitchen Tool Set: Made of heavy gauge metal with Russetwood handles. Convenient wall rack.

Cutlery

Saladmaster offers a complete line of fine cutlery designed by master craftsmen and executed in the finest stainless steel. Razor-sharp cutting surfaces feature the FIVE-STAR micro-edge, flat edge and hollow-ground edge for lasting service. Each knife is perfectly balanced for ease of use. All cutlery has Russetwood handles.

Steak Knife Set: This meat-cutting set is perfect for pork chops, chicken filets or a big juicy steak. Eight piece set available with rack or "butcher block" holder.

Hunting and Filet Knife: The perfect combination for the avid hunter and fisherman. Made of 440A steel that is both sturdy and flexible to satisfy the most discriminating person.

2-Piece Stellar Set: This 2-piece set features the all-purpose kitchen shear for trimming meats and a regular paring knife.

3-Piece Apollo Set: This ensemble includes a chef's paring knife, snack knife, and the 4 3/4-inch trimmer. Perfect for a gift or those smaller jobs around the kitchen.

2-Piece Vista Set: What better way to start your new cutlery collection than with a regular paring knife and a 7-inch carving knife.

5-piece Satellite Set: A collection of individually designed special purpose knives: regular paring knife, carver trimmer, butcher knife, French chef knife and 10-inch slicer.

3-Piece Carving Set: This beautiful carving set contains 9-inch carving knife with hollow-ground edge which can be sharpened to a keen razor-sharp edge. Gourmet fork, with curved shank, gives more control and strength when removing foods after cooking. The 7-inch carver is perfect for small roasts and hams.

Index

R eferences are to chapter and page numbers. For example, *Barbecue Chicken Wings* would be found in Chapter 1 on Page 6.

Favorite Recipes

Favorite Recipes

Favorite Recipes

Favorite Recipes

Favorite Recipes

Favorite Recipes

Favorite Recipes

Favorite Recipes

Favorite Recipes